Surveying the Domesday Book

by
Simon Keith

WIND*gather*
PRESS

Windgather Press is an imprint of Oxbow Books

Published in the United Kingdom in 2022 by
OXBOW BOOKS
The Old Music Hall, 106–108 Cowley Road, Oxford, OX4 1JE

and in the United States by
OXBOW BOOKS
1950 Lawrence Road, Havertown, PA 19083

© Windgather Press and Simon Keith 2022

Paperback Edition: ISBN 978-1-91442-710-7
Digital Edition: ISBN 978-1-91442-711-4 (epub)

A CIP record for this book is available from the British Library

All rights reserved. No part of this book may be reproduced or transmitted in any form or by any means, electronic or mechanical including photocopying, recording or by any information storage and retrieval system, without permission from the publisher in writing.

Printed in the United Kingdom by Short Run Press

Typeset in India by Lapiz Digital Services, Chennai.

For a complete list of Windgather titles, please contact:

United Kingdom	United States of America
OXBOW BOOKS	OXBOW BOOKS
Telephone (01865) 241249	Telephone (610) 853-9131, Fax (610) 853-9146
Email: oxbow@oxbowbooks.com	Email: queries@casemateacademic.com
www.oxbowbooks.com	www.casemateacademic.com/oxbow

Oxbow Books is part of the Casemate group

Cover illustration by Kit Keith-Reeves

Contents

List of boxes, figures and tables   vi
Glossary of terms   viii
Abbreviations   x
Acknowledgements   x
Summary   xi
Preface   xii

1. A surveyor's perspective   1
    1.1 Property list   1
    1.2 Opinions and anachronisms   4
    1.3 Agricultural land tenure   6
    1.4 Hierarchy of demesnes   8
    1.5 Quota and quantum taxes   9
    1.6 Consistency   10
    1.7 Geographic focus of the study   10
    1.8 Basic facts   11
    1.9 Mass appraisal   12
    1.10 Timescale: first subjective expectations   13
2. Why was the Domesday survey undertaken?   14
    2.1 The issues   14
    2.2 The options   14
    2.3 Is the Domesday survey a land register?   16
    2.4 Estate terriers   19
    2.5 Valuation lists for taxation   21
    2.6 The opinions of others   22
    2.7 The political incentives   23
    2.8 Conclusions about the purpose of the survey   24
3. What does Domesday record?   25
    3.1 The two essential elements   25
    3.2 Continual changes   26
    3.3 Comparing Domesday with other evidence   27
    3.4 The geographical ownership patterns   27
    3.5 What are the *ad valorem* property tax options?   29
    3.6 An analysis of the data   31

Contents

3.7 No hidden evidence	35
3.8 Summary of procedures	35
3.9 Hides and ploughlands	36
3.10 What was omitted from the survey?	39
3.11 No dwelling houses	39
3.12 No agricultural buildings	41
3.13 No other buildings	41
3.14 Recording other supporting agricultural assets	42
3.15 Non-agricultural assets	42
3.16 Resulting restricted tax base	43
3.17 Identifying the underlying philosophy	43
3.18 Woodland	45
3.19 Summary of what is assessed	48
3.20 Rationale for focus on arable land	48
3.21 The hide	49
4. Valuation	**55**
4.1 Annual sums and not capital values	55
4.2 What annual sums?	55
4.3 Rents and renting	59
4.4 Rental value or rent passing	60
4.5 *Ad firmam*	61
4.6 Actual or potential ploughlands	62
4.7 Rental values	64
4.8 Rental value dispersion	65
4.9 The main factors	65
4.10 Soil and land quality	68
4.11 Assessing agricultural potential	69
4.12 Exceptions and anomalies	71
4.13 King's direct holdings	71
4.14 TRE assessments	72
4.15 Assessments when acquired	74
4.16 Quality of the assets	75
4.17 Unresolved problems: summary	76
4.18 Determining rental levels in Domesday	76
4.19 No clear valuation method	77
4.20 Summarised basis of how the manors were assessed	78
5. The Boroughs	**79**
5.1 Difficulties of analysis	79
5.2 Summary of borough analyses	82
5.3 Comparison with Burghal Hidages	83

	5.4 Collecting the information	83
	5.5 Use and purpose	84
	5.6 Incomplete record	84
6.	The logistics	85
	6.1 The logistic framework	85
	6.2 Logistical issues	87
	6.3 Physical inspections	88
	6.4 The sequence of events	94
	6.5 The ICC as a precedent	95
	6.6 Preparatory stages before the fieldwork	98
	6.7 Logistics of the field surveys	99
	6.8 Logistics of judicial hearings	100
	6.9 The logistics of the editing and production of the written list	101
	6.10 Modern comparisons	102
	6.11 Size of the task	102
	6.12 The constraints	102
	6.13 The calculations	103
	6.14 Conclusions about timetable	103
7.	Conclusions	105
	7.1 What did Domesday achieve?	105
	7.2 Domesday considered in the historic context of taxation	106
	7.3 Narrow focus of Domesday	110
	7.4 Reflections on value	111
	7.5 Reflections on the logistics and timetable	111
	7.6 Final summary	112

Appendix A. Agricultural and estate management in the 11th century	115
Appendix B. Agricultural labour and the Domesday survey	121
Appendix C. Agriculture, livestock and land use	127
Appendix D. Landholders and totals	135
Appendix E. Cornish comparison	137
Appendix F. Capital sales evidence	140
Appendix G. Cambridgeshire Shire Reeve Picot's property empire	142
Appendix H. Surveying a village	144

Bibliography   146
Index   148

List of boxes

Box 1 A Domesday example or the village of Gamlingay in Cambridgeshire	xiii
Box 2 Taxation before title	19
Box 3 Hides: a system in use	38
Box 4 Land value taxation	44
Box 5 The Napoleonic cadastre in France	58
Box 6 Land measurement in the 11th century	70
Box 7 Stocking rates on unimproved land	128

List of figures

Figure 1 The Domesday survey geography	5
Figure 2 The basic structure	36
Figure 3 Oxen ploughing	37
Figure 4 Six hidage assessments in Bede shown in Table 8	51
Figure 5 Ten county boroughs	67
Figure 6 Location of seven boroughs	81
Figure 7 The vills in Armingford Hundred	94

List of tables

Table 1 A hierarchy of land holdings	8
Table 2 Numbers of main study areas	11
Table 3 Tenants in eight vills in Cambridgeshire	28
Table 4 Odsey Hundred in Hertfordshire	28
Table 5 Periodic property taxation options	30
Table 6 Structure of typical Domesday entry for each manor	34
Table 7 Six Cambridgeshire Hundreds with reduced hides	37

List of tables vii

Table 8 Bede: Some references to hide in the *Ecclesiastical History of the English People*	50
Table 9 Correlations of ploughlands or hides to £s per plough	63
Table 10 Value and distance from London	66
Table 11 Comparing the Royal holdings	71
Table 12 Comparing Cambridgeshire TRE with 1086 values	73
Table 13 Selected figures from seven Boroughs	80
Table 14 Valuation list logistics: a general framework	86
Table 15 Logistics and supplies	88
Table 16 Armingford Hundred comparisons	96
Table 17 Minimum manpower and timings for field visits to all vills	99
Table 18 Manpower and timings required for judicial hearings in each Hundred	100
Table 19 Volume of Work for Writing List	103
Table 20 Elapsed time	104
Table 21 A taxation comparison	107
Table 22 Domesday recorded numbers for Armingford and Clavering	121
Table 23 Estimated numbers for Armingford and Clavering as if in 1950s	122
Table 24 Numbers required for Armingford and Clavering in 1086	122
Table 25 The basic figures for livestock and land use in Armingford and Clavering	127
Table 26 GLU Ratios	128
Table 27 Calculations of land use for Armingford and Clavering	133
Table 28 Landholders in Cambridgeshire	136
Table 29 Landholders in Huntingdonshire	136
Table 30 Cornwall, selected statistics	137
Table 31 Sales transactions in *Liber Eliensis* (Fairweather 2005)	141
Table 32 Picot's sources of revenue	142

Glossary of terms

Term (as used in this work)	Latin (where applicable to the Domesday text and/or as transcribed in the Phillimore editions)	Definition or meaning (as used in this work)
Acre	acs (abbreviation)	Land measure of area being 4840 square yards or ten square chains or about 4047 m². Where the Domesday survey uses the term 'acre', the exact area is not known. It is often taken to represent a day's ploughing.
Ad valorem		Relating to value. In this work a tax that relates the value of real property.
Borough	Bergum	There are 112 urban settlements legally designated as boroughs as listed in the Domesday survey.
Bovate	bou (abbreviation)	An eighth of a hide, about 15 acres.
Cadastre		A register of property to serve as a basis of taxation.
Cambridgeshire	grentebrscire	The county as it was before 1974 which then did not include Huntingdonshire.
Chain		A linear measure: 22 yards. About 20 m.
Carucate		The Danish term for a hide.
Demesne	Dnio (abbreviated)	Sometimes used to indicate land in a manor farmed directly. Sometimes to indicate the entire estate of a landowner.
Estate Terrier		A register of the lands belonging to a landowner, originally including a list of tenants, their holdings, and the rents paid; later consisting of descriptions of the acreage and boundaries of all the properties. The purpose is to facilitate the management of the estate.
Furlong		A linear measure: 10 chains or 220 yards. About 200 m.
Geld	Geldum, geld (abbreviation)	A tax. Particularly in the context of Domesday, a tax raised to pay tribute to the Viking raiders based on a percentage, expressed as the number of shillings, of the assessment of hides: known as danegeld.
Great Domesday		The Domesday survey excluding Little Domesday.
Hide	hid (abbreviation)	An English unit of land measurement. Often considered to be equivalent to an area of about 120 acres, but variable.
Hidage assessment		The assessed number of hides ascribed to each manor, Hundred or county.

Glossary of terms

Term (as used in this work)	Latin (where applicable to the Domesday text and/or as transcribed in the Phillimore editions)	Definition or meaning (as used in this work)
Hundred	*hund* (abbreviation)	A Hundred was an administrative division of a county; often about 100 hides.
Huntingdonshire	*huntedunscire*	The county as it was before 1974.
In-hand		A term used to denote land that is not let. It is used in this work where the term *demesne* might not clarify the status.
League	*leu* (abbreviation)	A linear measure: 12 furlongs or 1½ miles. About 2.4 km.
Little Domesday		A separately bound part of the Domesday survey containing the counties of Norfolk, Suffolk and Essex.
Mancus		A gold coin currency.
Manor	*Manerium*	For Domesday it is the basic unit of assessment. More broadly, a manor is an estate in land to which is incident the right to hold a court termed court baron; that is to say, a manorial court.
Plough-land	*car* (abbreviation)	A taxable unit; approximately the amount of land which could be ploughed by a plough-team in the course of the year.
Pounds, shillings and pence. £.s.d	lib, sol, den (abbreviations)	The system of money as it was before 1972, with 20 shillings (s) to the pound and 12 pence (d) to the shilling; thus, 240d to the pound.
Rack rent		Open market rent or rental value. In this work the term 'rent' is a return or payment made in money or kind by a tenant to a landlord for the use of lands or houses. It is not here treated in the wider meaning used by economists.
Seneschal		A land administrative office. Not referred to in Domesday by this name but used in Norman French in medieval times. The office would have existed in 1086.
Shire Reeve		A royal official with responsibilities for the county.
Soke and Sake		Fines and other profits of justice relating to a manor.
Vill		The smallest administrative unit under the feudal system consisting of a number of houses and their adjacent lands, corresponding to the modern parish.
Virgate	*uirg* (abbreviation)	A quarter of a hide, about 30 acres.
Wapentake	*wapent* (abbreviation)	The equivalent of the hide for the counties under Danish rule during most of the 10th century.
Waste	*wasta* or *vasta*	Unused or devastated land

Abbreviations

DB	Domesday Book
ICC	*Inquisito Comitatus Cantabrigiensis*: A list of most of the Hundreds in Cambridgeshire in a format not dissimilar to the Domesday survey (Hamilton 1876)
IE	*Inquisito Eliensis*: An estate terrier for the lands of the Abbey of Ely (Hamilton 1876)
LDB	Little Domesday Book
MAFF	Ministry of Agriculture, Fisheries and Food
ONS	Office of National Statistics
TOR	Terms of Reference
TRE	*Tempore Regis Eduardi*: Domesday estimated related to the date in 1066 when King Edward reigned – i.e. on the eve of the Norman Conquest
VCH	Victoria County History

Acknowledgements

The starting point for this work was the introduction to the world of landscape archaeology that I received from Nick James and Sue Oosthuizen. I will always be grateful to them for opening this door to me. My former colleague Paul Sanderson kindly examined the first draft of this book and I greatly benefited from his comments, as I did from those of fellow Chartered Surveyor Alec Tompson, and Emily Phillips who examined later drafts. Tom Williamson was kind enough to give me his opinion, and his comments allowed me to see the viewpoint of a historian. Of course this does not imply that any of them agree with my interpretations of the Domesday survey.

I have enjoyed the constructive encouragement and support of all at Oxbow Books, particularly Julie Gardiner.

Sarah Wroot created all the maps. The base map including Armingford Hundred from 'An Atlas of Cambridgeshire and Huntingdonshire History' has been re-used with the kind permission of Anglia Ruskin University. Other maps include information from https://en.wikipedia.org/wiki/File:DomesdayCountyCircuitsMap.png used under the Creative Commons Attribution-Share Alike 4.0 International license. The additions and modification to the base maps are mine, as are all mistakes and errors. The image in Box 1 on p. xiii is by Professor John Palmer, George Slater and opendomesday.org and is used under the Creative Commons 3.0 Unported Licence (CC BY-SA 3.0) https://creativecommons.org/licenses/by/3.0/.

Summary

The Domesday survey was a property list carried out by men with surveying and valuation skills. This analysis of it, focusing on eastern England, has been carried out by a surveyor and valuer using the evidence contained in Domesday in comparison with other known property lists. Most of the logistical problems encountered by the Domesday surveyors are universal.

The main aim of this work is to calculate a timetable for the creation of the Domesday survey. In order to do so, it is necessary to analyse the text and to use 'reverse engineering' to determine the survey's purpose, what data was collected, the volume of it and how it was used.

The main conclusions resulting from the analysis are, first, that the aim and purpose of the Domesday survey must have been fiscal. It has the essential features of an *ad valorem* valuation list. The design and data gathered do not properly serve the only other feasible purposes which are an estate terrier or a land register. Secondly, Domesday was an agrarian list. The means of comparison and main determinant of value was the arable land. Other recorded items were generally relevant to a lesser extent to the valuation of the land. The survey was not a record of the built environment.

The significant figure in almost every manor was the 1086 valuation which was a rental value and not the rent passing. All manors must have been physically inspected during or not long before 1086. There is no known precedent for such a large amount of diverse data being collected, and judgements made, solely at judicial hearings. It is likely that plans had been made for the survey in the years before Christmas 1085. Logistical calculations indicate that it is just feasible, although unlikely, that all the physical surveys were made during the year 1086. The editing and writing of the survey would have taken much more than a year and the survey in the form we now have it would not have been available before the death of King William.

Domesday was a revaluation of the Hidage assessment system using the same underlying concept and the same administrative machinery but updating the data and adding monetary values. Although the survey provided a sound cadastre, it was never used to collect tax directly. It was therefore a fiscal failure.

Preface

The 1086 Domesday Book is of considerable historic significance. It is a large land-based list containing more than 250,000 facts recorded in more than a dozen categories. It covers an area of England of more than 44,000 square miles (114,000 km^2). It identifies more than 20,000 manors in 13,000 vills which mostly correspond well to modern parishes and thus almost every recorded item can be located within an area of on average less than 3 square miles.

It is a document that would be of value and interest in any age. Its antiquity makes it uniquely significant. There is a scarcity of written sources in 11th century Britain compared with later centuries and the Domesday survey fills a big gap. There is no other similar database extant for this period anywhere in Europe and probably nothing quite comparable in the World still surviving from the 11th century or before.

The Domesday survey is a rich mine of statistical information. It provides the historian with evidence of how England was governed after the 1066 Conquest. It provides for the geographer evidence of how resources were distributed. It reveals much about feudal England and the medieval agriculture which supported it. But the fascination for many is that it provides, through a narrow window, an intimate glimpse of life in their own village in 1086.

The Domesday Book is a list written in abbreviated medieval Latin and in that form is not easy for a non-specialist to read. It first became widely available from 1738 and, over the years, English translations, studies, analyses and commentaries have proliferated. Nevertheless, there is more to be said.

The purpose of this book is to analyse the 1086 Domesday survey with the perspective of a Chartered Surveyor and agricultural valuer in order to see if that point of view reveals any fresh insights. It does do so. Those who compiled the Domesday survey were the writer's professional precursors. The underlying theme of the work is to evaluate the logistical steps required to complete such an enterprise. This apparently simple and quite narrow aim became more complex during the process of this analysis. In order to calculate the logistics, the exact nature of each task has to be defined. Surprisingly, it is not always clear what the surveyors were recording and why, and how they used the captured data. This analysis sets out to identify the most likely probabilities.

The Domesday Book is primarily a national list of agrarian assets. A better understanding of it requires an examination of farming methods in the 11th century. Domesday itself reveals much about that agriculture. Other sources of information on medieval farming and land management are examined. They suggest an entirely recognisable agrarian landscape. In order to set the

Domesday Book in a wider fiscal context of similar records, it is compared to other cadastres, for property taxation, and property lists for two other purposes in several countries in different ages. In many ways Domesday was not unique when compared with later lists. All these comparisons are essential for a proper understanding of Domesday.

> ***Box 1. A Domesday example for the village of Gamlingay in Cambridgeshire***
>
> Gamlingay is a large vill in the Longstowe Hundred on the western border of Cambridgeshire next to Bedfordshire (NGR TL 2455). In 1086 Eudo held 90% of Gamlingay with two separate hides held by others. The parish was, until 1958 in size 4460 acres (1801 ha). The vill was probably similar in size in 1086. The soil is sandy, mainly derived from the Cretaceous Greensand. An ICC page which includes Gamlingay is missing.
>
> The Latin entry in Domesday is as follows.
>
> Phillimore's English Translation (Morris 1981, 25:9):
>
> > In Gamlingay Eudo holds 18 hides. Land for 18 ploughs. In lordship 9 hides; 3 ploughs there.
> > 30 villagers with 12 small holders have 15 ploughs. I Frenchman has ½ hide; 12 cottars; 4 slaves.
> > Meadow for 12 ploughs; woodland for 10 pigs; pasture for the village livestock.
> > Total value £18; when acquired £10; before 1066 as much.
> > Wulfmur of Eaton held this manor. 9 Freemen were there who held 4 hides; they could grant and sell; in addition to these hides they held 1 virgate which belongs to (Little) Gransden, the Abbot of Ely's manor, and which Lisois of Moutiers appropriated in the Abbot's despite, as the Hundred testifies.

Many of the topics covered and conclusions reached have been identified before by others although, in some cases, the methods of analysis here are new. Quantitative approaches are used where possible. The aim is that all the analyses and conclusions should be capable of falsification should better evidence become available. Some of the conclusions will not completely surprise those with a particular expertise of the Domesday Book. Some of the other conclusions do not accord with generally accepted opinions. The analyses result in different insights on several aspects of the survey and, in some instances, different interpretations.

The completion of the Domesday survey was indeed a remarkable logistical achievement. However, this study shows that it was narrowly restricted in its focus and not as comprehensive as many seem to suppose. Furthermore, unlike Danegeld levied under the earlier-established Hidage system, it was not a fiscal success.

CHAPTER I

A surveyor's perspective

1.1 Property list

The Domesday survey is a property list. Many of the practical problems and constraints encountered when compiling, maintaining and using such lists are universal in time and space and the same criteria would have applied then just as they do today.

The writer of this work is a Chartered Surveyor and valuer with five decades of experience of using, creating and designing property lists for tax, estate management and land registration in the UK and many other countries. This study seeks to use this first-hand knowledge of the practical difficulties encountered when either creating a new property list or maintaining or revising an existing one. How would these constraints have applied in 1086? This is the framework for this study. It uses judgements formed from anecdotal experiences acquired over several decades of a professional career. The writer has, on several occasions, been faced with essentially the same tasks as his professional precursors: the surveyors who compiled the Domesday Book. That same task is the compilation of a comprehensive, if selective, national property list. Of course, the modern surveyor now benefits from several advantages that the Domesday surveyors did not then possess: motorised transport, typewriters, tape measures and, usually but not always, maps. (In the first half of the writer's career, computers were not available and he knows from first-hand experience the problems of handling large quantities of data – relating to 25 million properties – without IT assistance). A professional understanding of the magnitude and complexity of their task cannot fail to produce admiration for the manner in which the Domesday surveyors carried out the work.

The initial purpose of this study is to identify a sequence of events that a surveyor undertaking the Domesday survey would have had to deal with. The next tasks are to examine the legal and logistical issues that would arise during the planning phase and then identify the problems of execution. The final task is to calculate the resources and produce a feasible timetable. This practical perspective adds a new dimension to the interpretation of the Domesday survey.

However, before any of the logistical problems can be considered the nature of the task of producing the Domesday survey has to be defined. Why was the survey undertaken? Exactly what information is being collected and how will it

2 *Surveying the Domesday Book*

be used? This requires a process of reverse engineering, i.e. using the final result to deduce the starting conditions at the beginning of the survey.[1]

The Domesday Book has been the subject of numerous painstaking studies by many eminent historians over more than 200 years: and interesting work continues. It is difficult not to be influenced and impressed by the enormous volume of fine scholarship. The quantity of words, statistical studies, analyses and opinions can be overwhelming and sometimes confusing. On some fundamental issues there is no general consensus. It is often tempting to be drawn into the arguments and disagreements but that is not the focus of this analysis.

Some bring particular expertise. F.W. Maitland (1989) viewed Domesday as a lawyer and mathematician. H.C. Darby (1977) was a geographer. Messrs McDonald and Snook (1985; 1986) brought much needed statistical methods with their analyses. This work brings another expertise. In spite of the sheer volume and variation of expertise in the commentaries, few of them examine the practical difficulties of the survey. Frequently, issues that would have been important to the practical completion of Domesday are overlooked or under-estimated. Then there are simple basic questions that must have been clearly determined at the outset for Domesday to succeed. These include the definition of a separately recorded unit, the bases of assessment and the method of valuation. The literature frequently does not address such fundamental underlying questions with the rigour and precision with which the organisers of Domesday would themselves certainly have had to apply. There is, then, surprisingly little comment on the fiscal impact, or the lack of fiscal impact, of the final list.

This work goes back to basics and examine the words and figures of the survey. The work seeks to use – and strictly interpret – the abundant evidence of the primary source which is Domesday itself. In some cases, this leads to the same conclusions as others, although sometimes for different reasons. In other cases, it provides a different perspective. For some issues, the conclusions run counter to accepted opinions. Using the ample evidence found in Domesday itself, this work provides a coherent, comprehensively reasoned view of how the Domesday survey was achieved. It takes into account logistical realities. It sets Domesday in context with other comparable property lists.

The intention is to provide conclusions that are capable of falsification, either on the basis of the evidence provided in this work, or with the advantage of better evidence mined from Domesday, or simply through contrary professional opinions.

The main historical sources are these.

i) The Phillimore Domesday county volumes of parallel Latin/English texts (Morris 1975–1986). Although the abbreviated Latin is noted, the study relies mainly on the English translations.

---

1   Others have used this approach for other topics. See for instance the study of the construction of the Baths of Caracalla in Rome (Delaine 1997)

ii) For comparison, reference is also made to the English Alecto translation by Williams and Martin (2003).
iii) For the *Inquisitio Comitatus Cantabrigiensis* (hereafter: ICC); the English translations in volume 1 of Cambridgeshire Victoria County History are used. (Otway-Ruthven 1938; Sulzman 1938, 400: 427)
iv) For *Liber Exoniensis* the information mainly comes from Weldon Finn (1960).
v) For *Inquisitio Eliensis* (hereafter: IE) the Latin transcription in Hamilton (1876) is used.
vi) For context and the perspective of a major clerical property holder in Cambridgeshire, an English translation of *Liber Eliensis* is used, particularly Book II (Fairweather 2005).

A reliance on the use of English translations is a potential weakness. Domesday is, in effect, a list written in abbreviated medieval Latin. To some extent the translations all render the text into full sentences or phrases and add words and punctuation that the translators consider are implied. There are also some variations in the different translations. The most important being those related to the abbreviation for *caruca*, or the Domesday abbreviation of it, which are rendered as 'plough(s)' in Phillimore and the Penguin translations (see bibliography). But they are 'plough-lands' and plough-teams in Darby (1977), 'teams' and 'teamlands' in Maitland (1989) and 'plough-teams' in Harvey (2014). The different terms used is indicative of the complexity of interpreting the meaning of the abbreviated Latin word 'car': a complexity that is not unravelled in this work. As this component is the central measurement unit of the document and crucial to the understanding of Domesday, the comprehension of its meaning is no matter of mere pedantry. The Latin in the survey is reasonably consistent in all counties. The abbreviated formula is often '*Tra e N car*' with abbreviation marks above the *Tr*, over the *e* and over the r in *car*. It is *Terra est N caruc*** with ending depending on the first declension case. It is usually translated as the dative. However, it is translated and whatever it means, the term mainly denotes a fiscal measure of comparison and not usually the instrument or team. That interpretation best fits the Domesday. Therefore the term 'ploughland' is mostly used in this work. This is not to say that the same Latin word is not sometimes and in some contexts in Domesday used to relate to the actual ploughs. The existence or absence of the plough, the tack and the ox team might well be strong evidence used to calculate the fiscal measure. In later centuries when some aides and subsidies, such as the 1/40th in 1232 and 1/30th in 1237 (Dowell 1965), were known to be based on chattels it may well have been that the actual plough-teams were a main asset on which those taxes were based. Furthermore, identifying it as a fiscal unit does not define exactly how that unit was measured.

There exists a handful of contemporary medieval comments on Domesday, such as those in the *Anglo-Saxon Chronicle*. Many more modern 19th and 20th century commentators on Domesday put great store on them, perhaps because contemporary written sources are so rare. Pollock and Maitland remark on rare written sources from this age as follows:

> This brings with it a temptation of some practical danger that of overrating both the trustworthiness of written documents and the importance of the matters they deal with as compared with other things for which the direct authority of the documents is wanting. (Pollock and Maitland 1959, vol. 1, 25)

As will be shown, these contemporary comments are not always strictly accurate in relation to the text of Domesday and may not necessarily be accurate in relation to other matters.

This work is essentially concerned with the administrative stages and procedures leading to the production of the Domesday Book sometime after 1086. This is an analysis of the many administrative processes that resulted in this document which was extraordinary for that era. The analyses and conclusions are mainly influenced by those geographic parts of the Domesday survey particularly studied here, albeit with the advantage of a general professional knowledge of real property, real property markets, real property lists and agriculture. The conclusions are based on the text of certain parts of Domesday and do not seek to go much beyond the reading and analysis of the Domesday texts, the ICC, Exeter survey and IE. These sources provide a substantial body of evidence.

Some issues are not much addressed here. Important though they might be, there are no comments or analyses of scutage, military or other services that ran with the land because they are not usually mentioned in Domesday and, when they are, it is usually obligations to the king and not to their own feudal lord. It is recognised that they were an essential component of medieval land tenure but apparently were not the central part of the narrowly focused Domesday list.

This work sets out a comprehensive and cohesive examination of how the considerable Domesday task was achieved logistically and how long it took. The analysis is set in the context of the history of taxation and the practical difficulties that the Domesday surveyors must have encountered. This analysis looks through a narrow window. Historians with a profound and extensive historical knowledge of the early medieval age and the feudal system will look through a wider window and be better able to judge the wider historical significance, if any, of these analyses; and whether they lead to a better understanding of that age.

1.2 Opinions and anachronisms

The bases of the analyses presented here are the many facts and numbers as stated in Domesday: there are about 350,000 of them. All the opinions expressed here are related to the Domesday survey facts which are supported by 1) tables of analysis (containing more than 8000 samples from which most of the tables in this work are derived); 2) the many numbers in the works of Maitland (1989), Darby (1977) and others; or 3) references which are capable of further

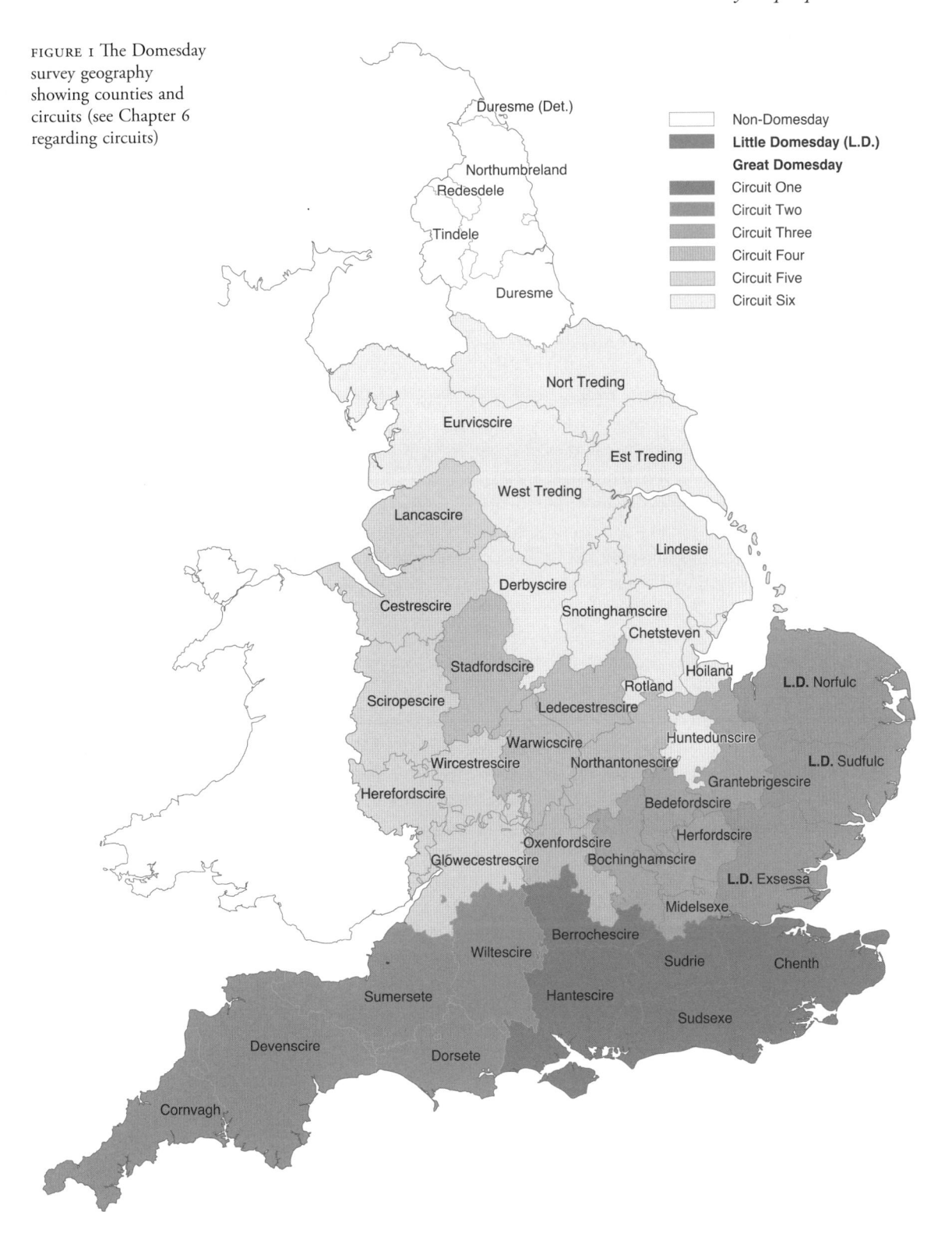

FIGURE 1 The Domesday survey geography showing counties and circuits (see Chapter 6 regarding circuits)

critical analysis by others. These facts or conclusions are then passed through the sieve of the writer's professional experience and own opinions for which there are fewer specific written sources in the public domain.[2] In interpreting Domesday there are the writer's views expressed on matters of valuation, estate management, property taxation, property law, agriculture and forestry. These views are there to be affirmed, falsified or modified by those with expertise and experience in these particular fields.

Every historian, to a greater or lesser extent, consciously or unconsciously, brings with them the perspectives and judgements of their own era. This work does so by its very nature. It uses 21st century professional knowledge of property lists to the examination and analysis of this 11th century document. Sometimes it uses modern terms and concepts to describe issues in a manner that would not have been familiar to the Domesday men carrying out the work. For instance, this work often refers to those whose task was to assess the manors as 'surveyors'. That term would not have been familiar to them but they were indeed surveying and valuing in a manner entirely familiar to the writer. The view is also inevitably subjective because the writer seeks to put himself in the shoes of the Domesday surveyors in order to understand the problems they had to overcome. The following sections are derived from the writer's 50 years professional experience and illustrate his mind-set – and perhaps his prejudices – in relation to some of the issues found in the text of Domesday or matters relevant to the creation of it.

1.3 Agricultural land tenure

Agricultural tenure is central to the Domesday Book. The tenure of agricultural land is, and always has been, varied and complicated. Agricultural land can be owned or leased or occupied or farmed under a wide variety of forms of tenure or licence. There is a broad continuum of tenures, from insecure short-term personal contracts, to enduring state-guaranteed property rights. Such arrangements can be:

---

2   These are all well-established disciplines, such as agriculture, forestry, valuation, surveying and estate management with their own body of established work and practices which this book frequently follows, often without specific references. The writer's opinions related to valuation and other estate management and taxation related matters are more difficult to back up with specific references or examples. There is, or there was, a large amount of written work by the writer in the form of many reports relating to many countries written over several decades. Most of these were never in the public domain and are mostly now not preserved, or else incorporated in other reports. These are mostly still not in the public domain, although many resulted in successful long-completed projects. For these reasons it is sometimes difficult to make specific references. Some more general works written or partly written by the author or commissioned by him are in the public domain (Keith 1993; and some of the FAO Land Tenure Series publications from 1997 to 2008).

i) land farmed under ownership with the farmer having complete control and taking all the profits and subject to all the risks;
ii) land leased to farmers for long or short terms of years, or life or lives, with the tenants taking the agricultural risks;
iii) land farmed in partnership with shared risks;
iv) share-cropping arrangements, exploitative or otherwise; and
v) short-term one-crop or seasonal grazing licences.

There are many other permutations and such a list is not exhaustive. It does not touch on common rights appertaining to land which, in some circumstances, are central to the local farming practices.

Evidence from countries throughout the world shows that, other things being equal, there will be a multiplicity of such arrangements, often with a bewildering diversity of local variations. The consequences for society are considerable. Land tenure not only affects land; the structures of society and land tenure are closely related. Such is clearly the case today with, for instance, much of the customary tenure in sub-Saharan Africa, just as it was for the feudal system in the 11th century England and Europe. The agricultural tenure situation in every country is further complicated by many family arrangements. Farmers the world over seek to keep the ownership or occupation of land within the family. Land is often farmed through loose family arrangements (Ravenscroft 2001).

Complexity is the norm. It is almost always difficult for an outsider to understand in the first instance the real land tenure situation and the true operation of land markets in another country. Things seldom turn out to be as they first appear, or even as law and/or custom decrees that they should be. Historians may well encounter the same difficulties when seeking to understand land tenure in previous ages. In recent years, in more developed societies, there is a tendency to simplify and codify land tenure, as has occurred in England and Wales with the *Law of Property Act* 1925 and related legislation. The occupational options may be further reduced by statute as was the case from the coming into force of the *Agricultural Holdings Act* 1948, until those strict security of tenure provisions were modified in 1996. Such simplifications are not the historic norm.

There is no reason to suppose that in England in 1086 agricultural land tenure arrangements were simple or homogeneous throughout the country. Tenure was very likely complex and varied, just as might be expected in any established landscape. This complexity has indeed been recognised and analysed by many historians such as Seebohn (1905). Domesday can only give hints of the variations because clearly the purpose of the survey was to simplify and codify the information. The aim was to force all these variations into a common, nationally comparable formula, and this was successfully achieved. The task would have been impossible otherwise and the final document of little use if the commissioners had not succeeded. As will be argued below, the essential underlying aim was to identify those that had the capacity to pay. The Domesday commissioners were probably not too concerned for their valuations with the many different ways the manors might manage their own lands or the tenure relationships with their villagers. Indeed, these tenure arrangements would have been continually changing and would have had little direct effect on the ability to pay.

1.4 Hierarchy of demesnes

We may be sure that the tenure situation in 1086 was complex. It is not a simple question of what was demesne land and what was not. The word demesne is often used loosely by commentators on the survey, and perhaps also in 1086. In the Domesday Book, the ICC, and the IE, a hierarchy of tenures is recognised, as shown in Table 1.

This framework is no doubt a simplification of the status on the ground. None of those five categories would have been permanent and the survey records either the legal or the *de facto* occupational circumstances at some date in, or just before, 1086. Category 5 over-simplifies the complex social, territorial and economic relationships inherent in these categories. The different categories were feudally significant and of great historical interest. They are less relevant to this analysis.

It should not be supposed that the named tenants or sub-tenants in rows 2 and 4 of Table 1 were of low or peasant status. Many substantial men held sub-tenancies. For instance, in Cambridgeshire, Hardwin of Scales held 15 sub-tenancies in addition to being the tenant-in-chief for 57 other manors. We can be sure he was not personally ploughing the land. This shows that the management of large agricultural estates must have presented many administrative problems. These estates were formed of scattered lands in scattered holdings situated in every county, as was the case for the King; or in several counties as, for instance, Count Alan with 48 manors in Cambridgeshire alone; or even with multiple holdings, mainly in a single county, as with Picot's 42 manors and 20 sub-tenancies in Cambridgeshire. Wide geographical distribution and scattered holdings create problems for the farmer or estate manager. Estate management and agriculture need local 'hands-on' management if they are to succeed and yield a rent or profit. Local agricultural farming responsibilities must have been devolved in the cases in rows 1 and 3 in Table 1 (see also in Appendix A the role of the Seneschals). As neither the King nor Count Alan

TABLE 1. A hierarchy of land holdings

1	The King's manors farmed or managed in-hand
2	The King's manors let to named tenants
3	Manors held rent free from the King by the tenants-in-chief and farmed or managed in-hand
4	Manors held rent free from the King by the tenants-in-chief and let to named sub-tenants
5	Lands in all the above categories not in lordship and farmed by the various named categories of peasants

could have been personally farming their extensive in-hand lands, and Picot could not have personally managed the Royal demesne in Cambridgeshire and his own numerous holdings in the county, there must have been a hierarchy of devolved responsibilities, which the survey does not reveal.

1.5 Quota and quantum taxes

Although now in discussions of matters relating to taxation the distinction between taxes based on a *quota* system and those based on a *quantum* system is not much considered, it has relevance to understanding the Hidage assessment system and the Domesday survey; particularly if, as is argued here, the purpose of the survey was essentially fiscal. A quantum tax is one where the amount payable is fixed and predictable. Thus, the tithe was known to be one-tenth of the produce. The produce might vary from year to year, but the tithe fraction did not. The Papal tax – 'Peter's pence' – was 1d per hearth. The ill-fated poll taxes of 1377 *et seq.*, were determined at various rates per person depending on status. These were all quantum taxes.

Much later, in France, about a decade after the revolution of 1789, a Napoleonic cadastral tax was deliberately designed as a quantum tax as a reaction to the much-resented arbitrary and unpredictable quota taxes of the *Ancien Regime*. These had included particularly the *taille real*, levied at different annual rates by the King depending on his needs that year.[3] The *Ancien Regime* tax methods were considered unpredictable by the taxpayers. (The system was of course considered unfair for several other reasons).[4]

Hidage assessments, on which Danegeld was collected, were based on a quota system. The amount needed on each occasion was, we might suppose, determined centrally, apportioned to counties in accordance with the Hidage assessments and then further subdivided in the same way to Hundreds, and further on down the line to vills and to individual manors. The share of the burden was predictable but the amount payable in any particular year or taxable occasion was not. This was the norm for centuries for the collection of many central government taxes such as aides and subsidies. It was also the basis of the Rating system from at least the 17th century until more recent years. Rates were levied at so much in the pound in relation the rateable value of the Rating

---

3   Napoleonic France imposed the Cadastral tax on some of the countries it had conquered before introducing it in France. Thus, it was applied in the Netherlands with the cadastral survey starting there in 1806 and taking 26 years to complete. It was not commenced until 3 years later in France, and then took 40 years and was never fully completed.

4   There were many other grievances relating to the tax system of the *Ancien Regime*. These included the fact that the taxpayers (for most taxes) did not include the aristocracy or the clergy and also the harsh administration of the tax system with more than 50% of the taxes being farmed out to powerful tax-farmers. Domesday made no such errors.

district according to the annual needs of the parish or other local body (such as the Poor Law Unions) for that year. The pure quota system for taxation now hardly survives in the UK except as the means of financing Internal Drainage Boards under *The Land Drainage Act* 1930.

It can reasonably be supposed that the Domesday assessments were intended, like the Hidage system, as the basis for a quota tax and the values are the means whereby the burden of taxation would be apportioned. At least the owners of the manors would have expected that this would be the case. This distinction between the two classes of taxes is important in any consideration of Domesday. When a quota tax was applied, it was in the interests of each landowner to see that other landowners in the Hundred were included, and correctly assessed. If one owner was omitted or under-assessed, a greater burden fell (or might fall) on the other correctly assessed landowners. The system was to this extent self-policing, as was the Rating system in later years. It is suggested that this factor accounts in large part for the relative accuracy and completeness of Domesday.

1.6 Consistency

All property lists, whether valuation lists, estate terriers or land registers, aim to be accurate, consistent and complete within their own terms of reference. Such perfection for any list the size of Domesday is an ideal that is never fully achieved. This is hardly likely to be publicly mentioned by the compilers of such lists. More recently, appeal systems exist to correct the inevitable errors. The Domesday survey is remarkable in that the great majority of the entries follow what is a clearly defined format. But there must be omissions, which are now not easily identifiable. There will certainly be clerical errors. There will also be matters recorded that are not relevant to the purpose and format of the survey which somehow escaped the otherwise ruthless editing and condensing process. Such things occur in any property list. Sometimes these Domesday inconsistencies might hint at something historically significant. Sometimes they might be mere anomalies. They are often the subject of interesting and illuminating comments by Domesday scholars: see for instance Darby (1977) on the geography of these differences. These anomalies are not the main focus of this analysis. The focus is on the usual and normal pattern of the great majority of the entries for the manors. Notwithstanding any such errors and regional differences, Domesday is remarkable for its consistency of method and cohesion.

1.7 Geographic focus of the study

In order to better understand the task of gathering in the field the information recorded in the Domesday survey, analyses have been carried out using as sources mainly the Phillimore county editions (Morris 1975; 1981; and others). All the entries in Cambridgeshire and Huntingdonshire have been analysed. The writer has carried out more detailed quantitative analyses in the Hundreds of Armingford and Toseland. The ICC has been analysed generally, but with a more detailed quantitative analysis of records for the Armingford Hundred and a comparison made with the Domesday entries for that Hundred. For a limited comparison with Little Domesday, an analysis of the entries for half Hundred of Clavering in Essex adjacent to Cambridgeshire has also been undertaken. The selection of these areas has no scientific basis. These are simply the counties and areas best known to the writer in a professional and personal capacity.

Domesday must be read and interpreted with knowledge of the landscape and the region being examined (or so it seems to a surveyor). They are all eastern counties, locations with similar if subtly different landscapes influenced by Jurassic and Cretaceous sedimentary strata dipping mainly east-south-east and extensively overlain by recent glacial till, particularly chalky Boulder Clay. Any analysis of other counties in, say, the north or the West Country (see Appendix E) with different geologies, climates, farming systems and histories will show different results in the detail. Cornwall, in Appendix E, is examined but in less detail. The broad conclusions have been checked against other areas known to the writer. These include Dorset, north Nottinghamshire, Herefordshire and Suffolk. Although the detail varies, the essential shape of Domesday does not.

1.8 Basic facts

The basic figures for the sample areas, and for comparison with the entire Domesday survey, are shown in Table 2. Other areas have been looked at but not with the same rigour.

TABLE 2. Numbers of main study areas

	Shires	*Hundreds*	*Vills*	*Entries*
CAMBRIDGESHIRE		16	145	446
Armingford Hundred			14	63
ICC for Armingford			14	53
HUNTINGDONSHIRE		4	90	140
Toseland Hundred			19	34
ESSEX		23	434	c. 900
Clavering half Hundred			10	19
ALL DOMESDAY	32	600	13,000	21,000

Notes:
i) The figures for Cambridgeshire and Huntingdonshire are from the writer's own count.
ii) The national figures for number of vills and entries are derived from the random sampling of more than 500 entries using the index in Williams and Martin (2003). The estimated figure of 13,000 vills accords approximately with the estimates of others.
iii) Using a national random sample, about 62% of the vills record only one manor. About 22% of the vills have two manors or separate entries recorded. In the remaining 15%, there are three or more manors or separate entries listed.
iv) The estimated number of Hundreds in the whole of Domesday is the weakest of the above figures.

It should be noted that:

i) The figures for Cambridgeshire and Huntingdonshire are from the writer's own count.
ii) The national figures for number of vills and entries are derived from the random sampling of more than 500 entries using the index in the Penguin *Domesday, A Complete Translation.* as the sample frame (Williams and Martin 2003). The estimated figure of 13,000 vills accords approximately with the estimates of others.
iii) Using a national random sample, about 62% of the vills record only one manor. About 22% of the vills have two manors or separate entries recorded. In the remaining 15%, there are three or more manors or separate entries listed.
iv) The estimated number of Hundreds in the whole of Domesday is the weakest of the above figures.

1.9 Mass appraisal

If there were potentially about 19 facts (as listed in Table 6 below) to be captured or estimates to made for each of the 21,000 manor entries, there are then more than 350,000 separate items of data to be recorded, discarded, estimated or captured in the whole of the Domesday survey. This may seem to be large number, but it is small by comparison with later surveys, such as that produced for the *Finance Act* 1909/10 for Increment Duty with about 10 million assessed properties, or Valuation Lists for Rating in the late 20th century with about 25 million rateable properties in England and Wales. When valuation lists, valuations or other property lists exceed the size at which one professional can personally control the content and quality of each of the entries, the organisational issues become as important as the technical ones. The organisational issues are in summary these:

1. Creating an accountable person, body or organisation or assigning responsibility to (an) existing body or organisation(s);
2. devolution of responsibilities within the assigned organisation(s);
3. devolving responsibility for specific tasks;
4. setting standards of consistency for recording, analysing and calculating data, and determining valuation guidelines;
5. planning the campaign;
6. executing and controlling the survey process;
7. making the valuations; and
8. editing and writing up the final list

This list illustrates that the entire process from beginning to end. It is complicated and time-consuming like most taxation administrative processes. Nevertheless, a large number of entries is not *per se* a problem if the resources, particularly persons trained to the correct level, can be deployed where required within the timeframe set for the task. This process for property taxes is commonly now called 'mass appraisal'.[5] The Domesday survey was an exercise of 'mass appraisal' and the eight stages above were all applicable and necessary and must have occurred.

1.10 Timescale: first subjective expectations

I would not normally expect any modern national or regional valuation list to be completed in much less than 3 years. That timescale is measured from the political decision to start the work to the finishing of the assessment task with the publication of the final valuation list. This time period would only be the case if the laws and the systems are already in place. In other words, I would normally expect a *revaluation* to take 3 years. Only then can tax collection commence. If there were no system in place, I would plan for a longer timescale. Such expectations are based on first-hand professional world-wide experience over half a century, reinforced by the recorded history of many other fiscal mass valuations and revaluations in the last hundred years. Many commentaries on Domesday seems to suggest that the whole project could be achieved in 1086. This is surprising as it is difficult to find any comparably short timetable for the completion of a property list of this scale. The collection of the field data for Domesday might perhaps have occurred in a very short period, mainly during the summer of 1086. The timescale for even this one phase would be a difficult achievement today and is remarkable when the logistics of the task in 1086 are considered. The shires furthest from London or Winchester lay at a distance of perhaps 2 weeks travel.[6] If this is so, even before making any detailed logistical analysis, it strongly implies that the Domesday survey was built on an already existing, sophisticated tax system. Even so, I would in the first instance still anticipate a 3-year timescale from start to finish. This subjective opinion was the main incentive that led to the more objective analysis that follows.

---

5   The process is now well suited to the application of IT and is known as 'computer assisted mass appraisal' or CAMA.

6   It would be difficult for a surveying/assessing team with horse transport to cover more than about 20 miles (*c.* 32 km) a day or say 120 miles (*c.* 200 km) in a week.

CHAPTER 2

Why was the Domesday survey undertaken?

2.1 The issues

Those charged with the creation of any property list need to be instructed on certain matters. For this conjectural project-planning exercise the following questions need to be answered before the organisational and logistical calculations can begin:

- What is the purpose of the survey?
- What are the nature and quality and quantity of the relevant data that is already known or recorded?
- What data have to be recaptured or reconfirmed?
- What, if any, new data must be captured in the field?
- How will the new data be captured?
- How will values be determined?
- How will the data be recorded?
- How will the data be interpreted?
- How will the data be verified/validated?
- How will the data be edited?
- What will be the final format of the document?

Each of these questions expands into several subsidiary parts. For this analysis we can summarise the issues into these simple questions:

- *WHY* is the survey being undertaken?
- *WHAT* is the taxable unit?
- *WHO* are the taxpayers?
- *WHAT* is to be recorded?
- *HOW* are the data to be interpreted and the values assessed?

These questions are addressed in the next chapters. They are relevant to the logistical calculations, but also to the general understanding of Domesday.

2.2 The options

The most basic and important question relates to the purpose of the survey. The first issue is whether Domesday had a single purpose. Many modern historians suggest it had more than one, perhaps misled by the notion that 'there is the indissoluble link between the payment of tax and title to land' (Bates 2018, 467). There is no such link.[1] A familiarity with the 600 year old Rating system in England, which is a tax on occupation not ownership, demonstrates this point on its own without looking any further. Others have suggested multiple purposes. Dyer (2009, 84) suggests three.

It is unlikely that it had more than one primary purpose. It is difficult to identify any successful property record anywhere at any time of this size that was commissioned for multiple purposes The Domesday survey is not unique in character and purpose: there were other comparable property lists before and after. It is unique in that it has survived so completely from that age. The main reason why a clear purpose is required is that conflicting objectives may well cause failure. Many attempts at property lists of this size, particularly cadastres for tax, fail.[2] When they do fail, they usually sink, leaving not a ripple on the surface water of history. If King William I had previously attempted to revise the Hidage assessment tax base and failed, we would probably have no record of it. Property records therefore are made for a single specific purpose although they may, and often do, later acquire a secondary use. If it is difficult to identify any (pre-IT) case where a property list was successfully completed for multiple purposes, why should we suppose Domesday was an exception? The surveyor or valuer needs to know the purpose for which any property list is being prepared. All valuations are purpose specific (see, for instance, the RICS Valuation Standards, 2014). Therefore, the first task is to determine what was the sole, or at least the primary, purpose of Domesday? This is a simple question to which at first there appears to be no simple answer.

There are now, and have been in the past, several different reasons for compiling property lists. There are three that are, by far, the most common and the only feasible options in 1086. Those purposes are these.[3]

---

1   It is beyond the intended scope of this work to examine in detail the dangers caused by legally linking too closely land registration to taxation. To do so weakens both systems: sometimes fatally. In brief summary, a tax liability linked to registration discourages owners from registering changes in title. The registration system then decays through lack of up-dating potentially at a rate of about 7% per annum compound. For taxation, it can also result in large areas of informal settlement being exempt from property tax. Informal settlements often include valuable properties. This is not simply theory. This is what actually happens in practice. There are, however, legal remedies that minimise the adverse effects.
2   During the writer's professional career he has seen attempts for at least four, and possibly six, major land taxation schemes in various countries either fail outright through a lack of technical expertise, and others aborted for political reasons, or which simply ground to a halt due to lack of political will or were completed so poorly that the results are useless.
3   There is another class of property lists: those that list of properties using or benefiting from a supply. Examples of such now include lists of those supplied with or using power, water, telephone, or IT services. Although none of these would be applicable in the 11th century in England, there had been user lists in existence

16   *Surveying the Domesday Book*

i. *Legal ownership*
   Lists compiled by the monarch or the State or other official body to record the legal ownership of real estate interests of others.
ii. *Estate management*
   Lists compiled for property owners for the management of their real estate. Such lists are usually termed 'estate terriers'.
iii. *Taxation*
   'Valuation lists' or 'valuation rolls' for the assessment and collection of annual or periodic property taxes.

All three types of lists can contain data in common. However, there are some data that are unique to each purpose. Land registers and Deeds Registers will have information related to the ownership or tenure of interests in land and the physical extent of it. That is their primary purpose. The information usually relates to the extent of the land only with no record of the buildings thereon. Land or Deeds registries will not contain information related to value, although they may contain the sale price of a property when last sold. An estate terrier will contain information about the extent of the estate ownership, including buildings and lease details, including rents. There will be subsidiary records, such as rent rolls, recording the amounts due and the amounts paid, where the lands are let.[4] It will probably not contain information about open market rental or capital values. Taxation lists will include an *assessed value* for each property. This is the primary purpose. It will contain the name of the taxpayer, and it will identify the taxable property.

2.3 Is the Domesday survey a land register?

There is a general historical progression of ways by which societies establish rights in land. In outline these start with:

i) oral grants, perhaps witnessed by others and often backed-up by customary physical ways of establishing and maintaining boundaries. For examples of this see Appendix F and Book II of *Liber Eliensis* (Fairweather 2015);
ii) individual written deeds and, thereafter;
iii) official deeds registers for the deposit of such individual written deeds; and
iv) lists, such as land registers, compiled officially to record ownership and protect private property rights in general and provide a guarantee from the state.

---

    for millennia previous to Domesday elsewhere. Irrigation systems covering multi-occupations required such lists so that the cost and benefits were shared *pro rata* amongst the users of irrigation water. In some Roman cities lists of private domestic and commercial water users were drawn up to charge for water usage in accordance with the size of the outlet (*calix*) from the local water tower.

4 See for example the *Inquisition Gheldi* in the Exeter Book (Welldon Finn 1964).

2. Why was the Domesday survey undertaken? 17

This is an over-simplified sketch and reality is usually much less tidy. We know that not all property transfers in the 11th century, in a largely illiterate society, were in writing. We can be certain that there were property disputes because this is the default state throughout the World and throughout history. Furthermore, the Domesday survey records many such.

It is difficult identify any national property lists in any country prepared for the purpose of regularising title before comparatively recent times. In Scotland, the deeds registers system – the Register of Sassines – dates from at least the 16th century and pre-dates any such system in England and Wales. It was one of the earliest. Effective though it was, it was not a universal list of properties but a record of land transactions. Land Registers, as we now understand them, are a comparatively modern concept, dating from the 19th century and are designed to extend the State's protection to private property. A much-quoted example is the Torrens system of Land Registration in Australia, commenced in the 19th century as a consequence of the allotment of land by the Crown for settlement. The underlying purpose of a land register in the last two centuries is to protect private property. In England and Wales, progress of the introduction of land registration has been slower because it is imposed on a long-since settled and established landscape. The Land Registry of England and Wales was still incomplete in 2017 and contained records for only 86% of the land area (HM Land Registry 2017).

It is commonly and erroneously supposed that before a property taxation system can be imposed there must already be a list of landowners in existence. In other words, it is sometimes wrongly supposed that full systematic land registration precedes land taxation. This is an incorrect assumption but understandable because, although the primary purpose of a valuation list is not that of assisting landowners and/or tenants to secure a title to their property, a taxation list needs a taxpayer attributed to every separately assessed plot of land. The taxpayer might be the owner, but this is not necessarily so in every system of taxation. It can be the person entitled to the usufruct or the occupier whatever his/her status.

It is suggested by Pollock and Maitland that, in Anglo-Saxon law, what we are looking at is not what we would now think of as ownership:

> Possession, not ownership is the leading conception; it is possession that had to be defended or recovered, and to possess without dispute, or by judicial award after a dispute real or feigned, is the only sure foundation and end of strife. (Pollock and Maitland 1959, vol 1, 57)

There are certainly indications in Domesday that it is recording and assessing the *de facto* possession of the properties.[5] Although the recording of legal title

---

5   This view is at odds with those of Welldon Finn in *Liber Exoniensis* (1964, 55) in his comments on *terrae occupatae* when he states that *occupare* conveys a suggestion of malpractice. This is not necessarily so. There are many circumstances in which the occupation may be within the law. Furthermore, the entire UK Rating system is

and tenure was not the primary purpose of Domesday, the surveyors clearly did get drawn into such matters. In five instances in Cambridgeshire and four in Huntingdonshire they record matters of irregularity or disputed title, almost as an afterthought. After the listing of other data and the financial figures for the entry, the survey records, in a few cases, disputes about title or complaints about alleged illegal acquisition of tenure of some lands or simple comments on previous tenants in chief. There is a lot of such material in ICC and Little Domesday.

In Huntingdonshire, at the end of that survey, there are also 29 declarations from those who gave evidence (*qui jurauer*) about matters of title. Some of them record matters in dispute. Others are records relevant to title. (It seems that those giving evidence were often keen to comment on matters of title. Ownership and occupation were, we might suppose, still very sensitive matters following the reallocation of so much land after 1066.) In no instance in those two shires do they determine a definite judgment about title. They only record the existence of a dispute or other alleged wrong and some of the facts as they believed them to be. They are a list of grievances. If the primary purpose was to determine matters of tenure it might be expected that a judicial determination, or at least a recommendation, would have been made on behalf of, or to, the monarch. The Domesday survey does not do so. Indeed, this would not be possible without hearing from all the parties involved. There are *de facto* two opinions in property disputes and we see only one side of them in Domesday. Matters of title are often contentious and seldom simple. Disputes can take years to determine. Such an exercise would be very expensive and bring no direct benefit to the Crown. It would have also brought to life many dormant disputes. The Domesday survey is not a land register nor is it an attempt to regularise titles because, quite simply, it makes no attempt to fulfil the primary function required of such a record. Lastly it should be noted that even where there is a dispute or an alleged illegal possession, it is the actual person in possession who is listed in Domesday as the tenant in chief. This conclusion is not challenged by the probability that the Domesday did, within about 100 years, acquire a secondary use as evidence of ownership.[6] Such a process is in accordance with historic norms.[7]

---

a tax on occupation rather than ownership. Perhaps Domesday foreshadowed this practice. There are good fiscal reasons for taxing the *de facto* occupier. A dispossessed owner has no resources from which to pay tax.

6   See, for instance, the reported words of Bishop Henry of Winchester (1096–1171) in *Dialogus de Scaccario* book 1:1.16, who said that its purpose was that every man should know his rights. See translation in Henderson (1896).

7   For two reasons there is some doubt about how much Domesday was in fact used as a basis to determine root title. First, 'there are only ten references extant specifically to the use of information connected with Domesday Book between the time it was made and the death of Henry I in 1135' (Clancy 2003, 33). Secondly, the first Statute of Westminster in 1275 specified *time immemorial* at 1189 and thus reset the

> **Box 2. Taxation before title**
>
> A strong case can be made that the historical norm is for registers first compiled for taxation to acquire over time a secondary use as the basis for evidence for claims to ownership. In other words, historically taxation registers almost always precede ownership registers.
>
> In some cases, the taxation register changes completely into a register of ownership and there are some well-documented examples of this process. This happened in the Indian sub-continent where the East India Company acquired from the Moghul rulers, after the battle of Plessy in 1757, a system of Land Revenue Taxation. It was a central part of the Company's, and later colonial, rule for several hundred years. The history of the colonial administration of the tax is not straightforward and the methods of collection were often harsh. Over the last 50 years, the fiscal purpose became less important. In Pakistan, by the 1990s, the collection of the tax had ceased completely but Land Revenue Taxation registers still existed at a village level and were maintained there by an official known as a *patwari*. These documents are used solely as a generally reliable register of ownership at a local level.
>
> In the Netherlands, Napoleon in 1806 imposed the newly designed (mainly agricultural) tax system collected on the basis of a detailed cadastre. It took 26 years to complete the cadastral survey in that country. The system changed gradually over the years from a taxation function to one related to ownership. Dutch Kadaster now administers a system that is a land register for the ownership of property interests and no longer has any connection with its original fiscal purpose.

2.4 Estate terriers

There is a difference between the lists prepared for taxation (by either central or local government) and those prepared for the purpose of estate management (whether the land is publicly or privately owned); such lists are termed 'estate terriers'. A primary function of a terrier is to keep a list of the properties that form part of that estate. We would now make a clear distinction between money received as rent and the values assessed for taxation purposes or the amounts actually levied for taxation. Estate terriers and associated documents such as rent rolls typically record the rents due and the amounts actually received. That is a main purpose. Such records do not usually record the full rental value, which

---

base date for title (and the establishment of other rights such as easements). If the Domesday survey was then widely used as proof of root title, we might guess that the date of *time immemorial* would have been set 100 years earlier at 1086.

may be more (and occasionally less) than the rent received. This is the initial reason why we might suppose that the Domesday survey was not primarily an estate terrier. It does not fit that purpose. Furthermore, if it was recording rents received, the results would not be as consistent as they are.

This does not completely dispose of the issue. First, we have the IE which is certainly an estate terrier, and has the purpose of listing the properties of that estate. It is prepared in a format similar to Domesday. However, it appears to be the case that the IE was prepared from the same sources as the ICC and perhaps some other lost sources (Weldon Finn 1960). In which case it is not surprising that the format is much the same. It simply re-used the Domesday data.

Secondly, this distinction between revenue from rent and tax might not have been so important in some ways to King William I because, after the Conquest, radical title for real property rested with the Crown, as is still the case today. In 1086 this was more than a legal nicety. From the Conquest onwards, King William and successive monarchs for more than 500 years have seen the whole of England as their estate; some of which was held by the tenants-in-chief rent-free (or freehold). In contrast, much of it was in hand and managed directly, although it is not clear how this was achieved. How much was done by the County Reeve and how much was he allowed to charge for this management service? How was the revenue audited? How did the crown keep central control of this enormous fragmented estate? How did the money flow from the county to some central point? There is little doubt that this management was generally effective.

But in other respects there was an important difference between the rents and geld taxation receipts. The king received the net revenues every year from the landed assets and matters he controlled. He received the rents from his in-hand land. At least this is the case after management costs. The levy of taxation, such as danegeld, was extraordinary and not a permanent annual event with geld being taken as a proportion of the assessment; that is the Hidage assessment or an assessed value. The political significance of this fundamental difference would develop over the years along the route to taxation-by-consent (at least tacit consent) with milestones such as the Magna Carta 1215, the English Civil War from 1642 and the American War of Independence from 1775.

The royal demesne revenue was the central source of state finance in the 11th century and would continue to be so for several centuries until it declined under the Tudors and the Stewarts (Braddick 1994). It might be supposed that the survey was in part useful for the management of the Royal Demesne.[8] In those Hundreds studied, the values per plough in the King's holdings are markedly higher than the mean (see 4.17 below). The full potential annual value, that is derived from the potential number of ploughlands, would be a useful tool

---

8   A distinction is made by Pollock and Maitland (1959, vol. 1, 383) between the 'ancient demesne' and land falling into royal hands temporarily through escheat and forfeiture and then being granted elsewhere. Such a distinction is not obvious in the Domesday survey.

for estate management. In fact, all the information in Domesday is valuable for estate management. It is suggested that, although the main purpose of the survey was fiscal, it probably also had some estate management function, at least for the Royal Demesne.

2.5 Valuation lists for taxation

Each entry in Domesday starts with fiscal data, that is to say, the Hidage assessment, and ends with the three values for that manor. The purpose of these values therefore appears at first sight to be fiscal. Perhaps this is why Maitland trenchantly expressed his view: 'Our record is no register of title, it is no feodary, it is no custumal, it is no rent roll: it is a tax book, a geld book' (Maitland 1989, 5). It could be argued that the existence of the *Inquisitio Gheldi* in the *Liber Exoniensis*, which is an account of what was paid or arrears that should have been paid, for the 6s geld of about 1083, reinforces this opinion. However, others later doubted this view (see Holt in the introduction to Maitland 1989; also Galbraith 1974).

For a valuer or legal draftsman, when reviewing, renovating or designing a periodic *ad valorem* property tax, there are three essential matters that must be included in any valuation list or valuation roll. These are:

i) the identification of the taxable unit,
ii) the identity of the taxpayer,
iii) the assessed value.

All these three essential matters are recorded in the Domesday survey for almost every entry. The exceptional instances for which this is not the case, when values are missing, are usually i) where the listed property is assessed with another entry, or ii) where the property is so small that the value is trivial, or iii) where the property has no value as it is waste.[9]

Although not essential, there are also other matters that are likely to be recorded in many valuation lists. Depending on local legislation and circumstances these might include:

i) an internal number for each entry within the valuation list,
ii) a short description or classification of the property,
iii) the name, and the identity and location of the occupier or tenant if the owner is not the taxpayer

---

[9] There are exceptions. See, for instance, the King's lands in Bassetlaw Wapentake in Nottinghamshire where, excluding mill values, only 18 out 64 manors have monetary entries. Some of these are clearly labelled waste and so considered valueless. Many others were almost certainly waste but not so labelled. Some are specifically assessed in other jurisdictions. Some are probably assessed with other jurisdictions but only by implication. Nevertheless, there are some omissions of 1086 values that are not readily explicable.

Most of these are absent from Domesday, but this would not impede its fiscal use. King William would have no difficulty in locating his tenants-in-chief. The County officials would know the location of the vills. In all the extensive commentaries and works on Domesday it is hard to find any that identify the three simple essential elements of an *ad valorem* property list. It is hard to make a judgement on the purpose of Domesday without these essential elements in mind.

In a modern valuation list, behind the bare statement of the assessed value, there is in the records a considerable amount of supporting information, the nature of which will depend on the type and size of the property. The data were and are used to calculate the assessed value. Almost all the information in the Domesday survey is entirely consistent with the type of information that a valuer would seek when valuing an agricultural unit.

Roffe says 'Neither Little Domesday Book nor Great Domesday Book lends itself for use as a geld book or directory of service' (2000, 242). Loyn says as follows: 'Domesday Book would drive the poor tax-collector to despair. For the taxman on the ground it was useless' (Erskine and Williams 2003, 22). I am that taxman and I disagree. The survey provides me with exactly the three essential items of information that I would require for each manor. I respectfully agree with Maitland. The purpose of Domesday was clearly fiscal.

2.6 The opinions of others

This work is not a critique of the many theories and scholarship written about the purpose of Domesday over last 150 years. The work does not seek to engage in a general discussion which would require a great many pages and distract from the reasoned conclusions of this analysis. The purpose is to start *de novo* from the original sources using a different expertise. The analyses in this work go back to basics: the large amount of evidence from Domesday itself. The works of others are not ignored. In addition to the writer's own counts, many of the facts and figures collected by others are used, particularly from the many tables in Maitland (1989) and Darby (1977).

There are three major issues that need comment from a broader perspective. First, lists of property made for taxation (*ad valorem* or on another basis) are common throughout history and throughout the World. Lists of properties created for fiscal purposes existed before 1086. Many such lists, valuation lists or valuation rolls or cadastres, are known in subsequent centuries (Dowell 1965, vol. 1). They are not uncommon. The other suggested options to explain the purpose of Domesday are not common. Why should we suppose that Domesday was exceptional. Common things are common.

Secondly, another opinion is that the purpose was to regularise title. This view is dealt with and rejected in 2.3, above. It is hard to find any national list with such a purpose in England or the World before the 18th century.

Thirdly some may think the purpose, at least in part, was to serve the feudal structure of society. It is difficult to find any other examples of such lists. The amount of detail in each entry about the classes and numbers of peasants listed in the manor, and attached to that manor, might give this theory some credence. However, the writer's view is that the persons are listed because they are attached to the land, either by law or custom, and therefore are relevant to the value of the manor. Domesday is concerned with land tenure. This analysis has little to say about the wealth of historically valuable information about the different peasant classes in Domesday. For the purpose of this work it is supposed that the agricultural output of a villain was no different from that of a serf. Furthermore, those listed do not constitute the entire available agricultural workforce (see Appendix B), nor do they represent the whole of the feudal hierarchy.

There are other matters that should be remembered when analysing Domesday. The first is that valuations are purpose specific, and there are valuation figures in Domesday for almost every manor. As previously stated, a valuation done for one purpose may not necessarily be of any relevance for another purpose. We can identify Domesday's purpose. It is fiscal. Domesday cannot be usefully analysed without determining its prime purpose. The second is that valuations are not of land or real property, but valuations of a legal interest in that land/real property. Domesday cannot be understood without identifying the legal interest. The exact legal interest relevant to Domesday will be identified in Chapter 3 below.

2.7 The political incentives

From a modern perspective Domesday was, by later standards, unusual in that it was a complete, thorough, national property survey that was accomplished without any particular tax or special geld having been specified beforehand, at least as far as we are aware. It is a tax base without any stated tax. It can reasonably be supposed that it was intended to replace the Hidage assessment system with a more accurate tax base. We can suppose that there was a perceived urgent need to defend against invasion.

This contrasts with other national property tax cadastres such as the Land Revenue Tax in the Indian subcontinent; the Napoleonic cadastres in several countries designed and introduced in the early 19th century; the English Land Tax assessments from 1696; the complete national survey in the UK carried out for Increment Duty under the *Finance Act* 1909/10; or later Rating valuation lists. The subsequent effectiveness of the originating taxes in these examples varied and not every one of those listed was a fiscal success. But, in those cases, the tax was specified in law *before* the surveys were commenced. It is the fiscal urgency that provides the political will and normally dictates the timetable and it is that factor that drives it on and causes the completion of the tax base. (Even fiscal urgency does not always result in success. There are many cases of failed attempts to introduce systems of taxation.) The collection of information for the survey was completed rapidly without a specific stated fiscal driver. This might be indication of four issues. First, there must have been a sense of urgency or danger that drove the project on to completion in such a short time. Secondly, it is evidence of the strong effective political will. Thirdly, at that time the clearly expressed royal will, at least of King William, was sufficient without any specific law. Fourthly it supports the thesis that Domesday survey was a development of the existing Hidage assessment system.

All taxation has a strong political dimension. Sometimes it is an overt means of control. This was certainly the case for the Land Revenue Tax in India levied first by the East India Company and, later from 1858, under the colonial rule of the India Office. Similarly, the Domesday survey would have had a significant political dimension. It must have been a compelling means of control over the powerful tenants in chief. Tenure was at the will of the King. The survey accurately revealed to him, and to those holding from him, who had the most to lose.

2.8 Conclusions about the purpose of the survey

The logic of the above excludes two of the three possible reasons for compiling Domesday. The conclusions broadly concur with the opinions of some but not all, and are these:

- The Domesday survey was not undertaken principally as a national record of land tenure. Such an exercise would have been very unusual at that period.
- Domesday was intended to be a fiscal list.
- As with taxation lists prepared in later ages, Domesday did, to some extent, later develop a secondary function as an indication of tenure.
- Domesday was not primarily an estate terrier. The survey would have some relevance to estate management particularly in relation to the King's Demesne.
- The most important entries in Domesday are those related to values.

CHAPTER 3

What does Domesday record?

3.1 The two essential elements

A fiscal property list requires clarity in respect of the definitions of two essential elements:

a) What is the unit of assessment?
b) Who is the taxpayer?

In most respects, the text of Domesday is clear and it may appear that the definition of each is simple and apparent. The Domesday surveyors, like those responsible for the Hidage assessments, would have well understood the importance of these two issues. It is unlikely that the answers in the field were always straightforward. The unit of assessment is clearly the manor assigned to its respective vill, whether in the Royal demesne or otherwise. However, it should not be assumed that the boundaries of every manor fell entirely within the bounds of the vill in which it is recorded. Sometimes this is clear from the Domesday entry.[1] It may well be that there were others where it was not thought necessary to record every outlier. Nor is it likely that the lands of a manor within that vill usually fell within a ring fence or be supposed that the manor necessarily must have included a manor house (see 3.11 below). The manor was a taxable land unit: one that would, in later ages, for Rating be called a 'hereditament'.

The persons primarily liable for tax, if it had been levied, would be the tenants-in-chief, as are listed in the counties, in most cases, after the listing of the boroughs. That is why they are identified there (see Appendix D). Of course, they might have attempted to pass the burden onto their sub-tenants or peasants. In fact, whatever they did, the resulting burden would, in reality, have remained with the tenants-in-chief because if the sub-tenants were made to carry the extra burden of tax, they could afford to pay less rent. There would be no net advantage accruing to the tenant-in-chief, at least this is so if rack rents were paid. The ultimate burden of a tax does not always come to rest where it first or apparently falls.

---

1 There are many examples. See for instance Dunham in Nottinghamshire (Morris 1977, 1.1) with four listed outliers: Ragnall, Wimpton, Darlton and Swanston. Although all these parishes/vills are contiguous, it is unlikely that all the lands were. See also in Essex a Manuden listing as part of Stansted Mounfitchet in the adjacent Hundred (Morris 1983, 2.16).

3.2 Continual changes

The statuses of tenancies shown in Table 2 above would not have been fixed and unchangeable. The production of any property list is like trying to hit a moving target. There are changes in ownerships and occupations happening all the time. They happen when the list is being compiled, after it has been compiled and before it comes into operation. Change continues to happen when the list is being used. In the 21,000 entries, there are references to at least 12,000 mortal individuals such as:

i)   tenants-in-chief,
ii) sub-tenants of the King,
iii) sub-tenants of the religious establishments, and
iv) tenants of the tenants-in-chief

There would be about 5%, or say 600, title changes during any one year, simply due to human life expectancy and the span of a working life. The villeins and other classes of peasant would also die and be changing, although Domesday would be less concerned with these as individuals. There were also other causes for change even within the Royal lands as Pollock and Maitland point out: 'The king is a great landowner. Besides being supreme lord of all lands, he has many manors of his own; there is a constant flow of lands into and out of the royal hands; they come by escheat and forfeiture, they leave by gifts and restoration (Maitland 1959, vol. 1, 383).[2]

Nor should we assume that the ownerships were fixed for ecclesiastic lands. In Domesday, the Abbot of Ely had in Cambridgeshire about 40 manors in hand and about 20 let to named sub-tenants; 12 of them to Hardwin of Scales and two to Picot. This was not necessarily what the brothers of Ely would have wanted as shown by a passage in *Liber Eliensis* written not long before King William's death, and referring to the records of the IE:

> ... the abbot, not of his own volition, and not from favouring the rich, or from fondness towards relatives, permitted usurpers, such as Picot the sheriff, Hardwin de Scalers, Roger Bigod, Hervey de Bourges, and others to hold certain lands of St AEthelthryth as the Book of Lands reveals, but none of them of terms of complete lordship. (Fairweather 2005, Book II, 134)

The Abbey of Ely, previous to the extract above, lost land after the upheavals caused by Hereward (and others). They got lands back perhaps between 1070 and 1080 as the following extract records:

> ... cause the Abbot of Ely to be put in possessions again of the following lands which the following people hold: Hugh de Montford a manor called Barcham; Richard, son of Earl Gilbert, Broxted; Picot the sheriff, Impington; Hugh de Berners, three hides;

---

2   It is not immediately apparent that the Domesday survey distinguishes between what Pollock and Maitland (1959) define as the ancient demesne and other perhaps more temporary Royal holdings.

Bishop Remigius, one hide; the Bishop of Bayeaux, two hides; Frodo, brother the abbot, one manor; the two carpenters, one hide and three virgates; providing they and can demonstrate that the aforesaid lands are from the demesne of his church and providing that the aforesaid men are unable to demonstrate that they held these lands as a gift from me. (Fairweather 2005, Book II, 122)

It might be supposed that the Domesday survey records the circumstances as at some date, probably 1086, when the vill was inspected, or perhaps when the circumstances were considered at a judicial hearing. By the time a fair copy of the list was written-up at least 10% of the entries would have been incorrect to some material extent.[3]

3.3 Comparing Domesday with other evidence

There is other evidence of land transactions in the 11th century, and later, recorded outside the Domesday survey. Commentators on occasions refer to them and they might sometimes throw light on the matching Domesday survey entries (Harvey 2014; Maitland 1989; and many others). The problem in making comparisons and/or deducing trends is that the written sources of the transactions may not exactly describe what was being recorded, conveyed, let or farmed. There are many permutations. We cannot be sure that the geographical extent of the manors remained fixed. We do not always know what rights were involved in these recorded transactions. It could be the agricultural land only; or all the land and buildings thereon; or all rights in land and buildings and soke and sake and other sources of income. The transaction might, or might not, include livestock, growing crops and other matters that would later be termed 'tenant right'. Furthermore, we may not know what common rights ran with the land. Did the consideration include timber? All these considerably affect the capital price of land, or the annual rental value, or the premium payable to farm it. Care should be taken in drawing conclusions from such transactions unless the nature of what was involved is known.[4]

3.4 The geographical ownership patterns

Domesday itself gives no indication of the exact geographical patterns of ownership and occupations within the manors. However, the holdings of the tenants-in-chief and their sub-tenants suggest a complicated pattern. We do not know the exact geographic boundaries of the Domesday ownerships but the indications are that many estates were made up of scattered parcels of land. For instance, there were 14 separate owners or tenants of rights in land in Cambridgeshire in the upper Rhee valley vills of Litlington, Bassingbourn,

---

3   We might guess that the rate of change continues at a compound rate of about 7% per annum.
4   As every valuer knows, valuations are not made of land or real property, but the value of a legal interest in that land or real property.

Wendy, Whaddon, Orwell, Shepreth, Meldreth and Melbourn in 1086. The three largest tenants in those eight vills are listed in Table 3.

Earl Roger also had other lands in Guilden Morden, Steeple Morden and Abington Pigotts which could not have been contiguous with his lands in the vills noted in Table 3. This suggests a complex pattern of ownerships and occupations for the tenants-in-chief and this pattern might well have been reflected in the occupations of manors within the vills (Keith 2017). The dispersion of holdings can be seen also in Table 4 of the Odsey Hundred in Hertfordshire (Morris 1976).

None of the manors in this Hundred lies within the King's estate. The balance of in-hand to let land is not untypical with, in this case, 68% of the value in-hand, in that there is no named sub-tenant (although much of the in-hand land of the tenants-in-chief was farmed by the villagers). Some of the sub-tenants have more than one holding in this Hundred. Theobald has five,

TABLE 3. Tenants in eight vills in Cambridgeshire

	Count Alan	Hardwin	Earl Roger
Litlington	T		
Bassingbourn	T	T	
Wendy	T	T	
Whaddon	T	T	
Orwell	T	T	T
Shepreth	T	T	
Meldreth	T	T	T
Melbourn	T	T	T

T = tenant with land in the vill

TABLE 4. Odsey Hundred in Hertfordshire

Item	Numbers
Manors in-hand	19
Manors with sub-tenants	23
Value of in-hand manors	£92
Value of let manors	£42
Plough-lands in-hand	103
Total number of manors	41
Other statistics	
Total number of hides in Hundred	121
Total number of plough-lands in Hundred	197
Total value in 1086	£134
Value TRE	£166

Osbern four and Withgar two. Clearly, they were substantial farmers with interests across vill boundaries.

The fragmentation and complexity of the occupations posed difficulties for the Domesday surveyors as they would for any other land surveyor. Ownership and occupations might well have been scattered in furlong strips in the two or three open fields. Not every furlong would be exactly 10 chains long and one wide. Not every boundary would be straight with the reverse S shapes being common in the furlongs. It is likely that the expertise to survey and measure such a fragmented landscape existed with nothing more sophisticated than a measuring rod or rope or chain. But such an exercise is very time consuming. It might well have been simpler in some cases to count the ploughs or listen to those giving evidence and make a judgement on that evidence.

In summary:

- The taxpayer was any tenant-in-chief holding rent free from the king.
- The manor was the unit of assessment.
- Manors were commonly sub-let and the pattern of such leases would have been continually changing.
- The manors and the lands held with the manors usually or commonly consisted of scattered plots and fields, at least in the 'champion' landscape.

3.5 What are the *ad valorem* property tax options?

If the primary purpose of Domesday was fiscal, how does the survey fit with a general view of *ad valorem* annual property taxes? The four basic options, and 32 theoretical permutations of them, for what assets are to be listed and how they are assessed for annual *ad valorem* property taxes are as shown in Table 5. Although in 1086 royal taxes were not then levied on an annual basis, but when revenue was needed, the same principles of assessment apply.

How does Domesday fit into these options? In respect of Issue 1, it is generally accepted that the monetary figures in the survey are, or relate to, an annual figure (and see discussion and comments in 4.1 below). For Issue 2, it is clear that the Domesday surveyors well understood the difference between existing use and optimum use. In 146 vills in Cambridgeshire and 90 vills in Huntingdonshire, in addition to the number of actual ploughlands (that is the existing use value), there are references to the number of ploughlands that could be supported in that manor which indicates the 'highest and best' use or optimum use. In the Armingford Hundred, 14 out of 62 manors have more potential ploughlands than those actually in arable use. The total potential ploughlands number 183 compared with 162 *actual* ploughlands. That Hundred is not untypical, at least not in the southern and eastern counties.

For Issue 3, the question of who pays is more difficult. Much later, the issue of who pays a real property tax was addressed by a church court for the Rating system in the case of *Jefferys* in 1596 when it was determined that liability for that tax lies with the occupier rather than the owner. The UK rating system

TABLE 5. Periodic property taxation options

Issue	Options	Some modern examples
1	*What* is the basis of assessment?	
	1.1 the rental/annual value, or	1.1 UK Rating system was rental value, and still is so for Business Rates
	1.2 The capital value	1.2 Many examples of capital value in the world, including USA
2	*What* is the underlying valuation assumption?	
	2.1 The 'existing use value', or	2.1 In the UK rating system is the existing use or *rebus sic stantibus* (matters standing)
	2.2 Optimum 'highest and best use'	2.2 It is highest and best in USA
3	*Who* pays?	
	3.1 Owner, or	3.1 In most countries it is the owner
	3.2 Occupier	3.2 UK is unusual in taxing the occupier
4	*What* is to be valued and assessed?	
	4.1 The land only, or	4.1 Kenya and other countries
	4.2 The land and the buildings thereon, or	4.2 UK and many countries
	4.3 The buildings only, or	4.3 Ghana
	4.4 All sources of income from the land	

and the Council Tax and Business Rates are still taxes on occupation. For the Hidage system – and presumably for subsequent central government taxes such as aides and subsidies – the liability devolved from the top with the tenants-in-chief being primarily liable. It seems, in practice, that the tenant-in-chief in *de facto* occupation or in control was treated as the taxpayer for Domesday, even when a dispute about title is recorded. Domesday is a list of those liable to be taxed. They are generally named in a list at the start of each county record.

Of course, the tenant-in-chief might seek to pass the tax liability down the line. If the tenant occupier is required to pay, he then has less ability to pay a rent – at least this is so if it is a rack rent – and the landowner bears the ultimate economic burden. In any case the primary liability for taxation remained with the tenant-in-chief.

It should be noted that in the *Inquisitio Gheldi*, in *Liber Exoniensis*, it appears that the lands in demesne (in-hand) were exempted from the 6s geld and that tax was paid from the lands of the *terrae villanorae,* which this writer translates as 'the lands of the villagers' (Weldon Finn 1964, 188). It seems unlikely that this was the norm although, on that occasion, it might have been a recognition that the tenants-in-chief owed particular service to the king.[5] It would certainly have reduced the tax yield. Such a general exemption opens the way to tax avoidance on a considerable scale; simply by taking land in-hand. Furthermore, the longer the exemption persisted, the larger the scale of the avoidance. It therefore seems unlikely that the Hidage system would have survived with such fiscal success for so long if there was such an avoidance

---

5   This was the reason in France for the aristocracy being exempt from the *taille* under the *Ancien Regime.*

defect in existence prior to the 6s geld. There is no indication that this exemption would have been part of the Domesday tax base after 1086. The survey does usually state the extent of the ploughlands in-hand and we can know the proportion of them as part of all ploughlands in the manor. But the meadow, pasture and woodland, and the Domesday values, are not then apportioned and it would have been difficult to do so using only the information recorded in the survey. There is no indication from the 1086 manor values that they exclude the value of the in-hand land.[6]

However, there were some other customary exemptions and one is listed in 'The Dialogue Concerning the Exchequer' in book 1 item 11 (Henderson 1896). In that paragraph 'What is Danegeld?', it states that the lands of the sheriff are exempt in return for the collection of the tax. If this is so, Picot in Cambridgeshire benefitted. As tenant-in-chief he owned 7.6% of the land by value and thus the cost of collection for his services alone was 7.6% of the county revenue. We might suppose that he only got paid for the money he actually collected. There were other costs of administration, assessment and collection, further up the line of command. There are also other exemptions listed. We can guess that the cost to yield ratio of a geld was at least 10% for Cambridgeshire. These figures relate to a normal geld. The Domesday revaluation was a large additional cost. It was an expensive undertaking. It might be possible to quantify this cost although this analysis does not attempt to do so.

3.6 An analysis of the data

What assets are being listed and assessed in the survey? The question can be answered by an analysis using the abundant evidence in Domesday and ICC and the *Liber Exoniensis* (Weldon Finn 1964; Roffe 2000, 94 and others). In broad terms, it was 'the land only' as in row 4.1 of Table 5. That is what the survey records in some detail. It does not list those matters related to the other options in row 4 of Table 5 – that is to say, the buildings. This is an issue that is important to the understanding of Domesday, and it seems the significance of it is not often appreciated.[7]

We can be more precise. There is a wealth of data and, for almost every manor, the listings follow a set pattern that must have been laid down somewhere in what we might now call a 'terms of reference'.

A 'terms of reference', i.e. a list of the data to be collected, is included in the IE, which is certainly an estate terrier and not a fiscal list:

What is the name of the manor?

---

6   For instance, the correlation of the ploughlands not-in-hand to 1086 values in Armingford is 0.88; in contrast to a correlation of 0.92 for all ploughlands to 1086 values. These figures are typical. If the values related only to the ploughlands not in-hand the correlation would show it.

7   Rackham is an exception. He correctly says 'Domesday is a record of land' (Rackham 1986, 14).

Who held it at the time of King Edward? Who holds it now?
How many hides?
How many ploughs in demesne – of the tenants?
How many villeins – cottars-slaves?
How many freemen-sokemen? How much wood-pasture?
How many mills-fisheries?
How much has been added or taken away?
How much was the whole worth? How much now?
How much had or has each freeman, sokeman?
All this to be given thrice: that is, in the time of King Edward, and when King William gave it, and at the present time.
And if more can be had now.
(Henderson 1896, 97)

This is often cited as the (or a) terms of reference for Domesday (hereafter IE/TOR). The above wording clearly sets out the degree of detail required and corresponds with many of the items of information recorded or captured. It is not clear why a terms of reference was recorded in the IE which was probably written after 1086 (Welldon Finn 1960). It appears that IE was derived from Domesday and post-dated it. It therefore adds little to the underlying analysis of Domesday. The IE/TOR ('terms of reference' if that is what they are) do not apply exactly to Domesday survey because, in the event, the information was not recorded in precisely that way. We can identify some differences.

i)   The manors are not named: although they are clearly identified by the name of tenant-in-chief and the vill in which they are recorded.
ii) The IE/TOR implies that all the data is captured for three dates, and that is not the case; although the values often are, but not always, captured thrice.
iii) The actual ploughlands of each manor are recorded in Domesday and sometimes then the potential ploughlands in that manor. The IE 'terms of reference' do not require this important second phase.
iv) Domesday does not record how much each freeman or sokeman had or has unless they are recorded as named sub-tenants in individual manor entries. This might be what the IE entry means.
v)   In Domesday, it does not usually list how much has been added or taken away; although there is similar sort of information about title in the ICC in many instances and quite a lot of such information in Little Domesday.
vi) The IE/TOR 'terms of reference' make no mention of livestock although such information is recorded in Little Domesday for two dates, in the ICC and in the Exeter Book; and we might suppose such data were captured in an original survey. If so, reference to livestock must have been in the real terms of reference and/or the instructions.
vii) The IE/TOR reference to wood-pasture is very broad brush and, in most counties, the survey distinguished between woodland, pasture and meadow (although this is not generally so in Nottinghamshire where it lists

wood pasture only). Meadows and grazing are significant, as Appendix C demonstrates.

Thus, the structure of the IE is not exactly the same as that in Great Domesday nor is it ordered as the structure of the ICC. The differences may appear small, but they are significant. Table 6 shows the Great Domesday structure of the typical entry for each taxable unit; which is the individual manor in a particular vill in the ownership or occupation of a named tenant or sub-tenant. Detail and accuracy are important in a national exercise such as Domesday. The actual structure for the great majority of manor entries as shown in Table 6 is well-defined and much more rational than that description in the IE.

The structure shown in Table 6 identifies what data the surveyors intended to capture, in potentially 19 separate fields and, in most cases, succeeded in capturing efficiently all that was necessary for that manor. There is other information randomly captured in some instances: for example, churches and saltworks. We might suppose that information about livestock was captured in the original survey. Row 4 is a fiscal measure and the main means of comparison. It should be noted that in rows 7 and 9 of Table 6 the question of whether the abbreviated Latin word *car* in those circumstances should be translated as 'plough-team', the fiscal unit of comparison, or 'plough'; the instrument is not answered because the writer does not know which is the case. The actual plough(s) may sometimes have been taken as an indication of the fiscal unit. Nevertheless, we can see the pattern of the assessment. There must have been clear and precise instructions which are now lost to us; and they are not those in the IE. This must be so because such consistency of method as is demonstrated in Great Domesday cannot happen by chance: and it is difficult to achieve in practice on this scale. There must have been a terms of reference or something similar. The whole enterprise must have been planned in clear and exact detail. Then, derived from the terms of reference, there must have been clear and precise instruction, and these instructions must have been successfully transmitted, orally or in writing, to all those gathering the information in the field or giving evidence. This was no small undertaking in itself. This would have been of particular importance where the execution of the survey was in anyway different to the well-established practices related to the assessment of the Hidage. There must also have been continuing vigorous supervision throughout the whole period of the work to enforce this consistency.

None of this ever happens accidentally. A lot of people were involved (see Chapter 6 below). They all have to be controlled and continuously monitored. We can be sure that this must have happened because we have the evidence of consistency in Domesday. It did not happen by random chance. Those with practical experience of gathering such information in the field cannot but be impressed by the results of such ruthless administrative competence. Those with practical experience of creating a tax base for an *ad valorem* property tax will recognise the administrative processes that must have been involved.

	Item recorded	Comment
1	IDENTITY OF TAXABLE PROPERTY. Name of tenant-in-chief (or King) and vill in which the manor is recorded	This identifies the taxable unit and the taxpayer. The manors are not otherwise described by the name of the manor itself in Domesday (nor in the ICC). The system exactly locates the Manor to a vill but not where in the vill the lands of that manor lay
2	Identify sub-tenant of manor if any	Applicable only if sub-let
3	ASSESSMENT IN HIDES	This is a fiscal starting point. The survey also records variations in the Hidage assessments, if any
4	NUMBER OF ACTUAL PLOUGHLANDS IN THE MANOR	This is a key figure
5	Number of potential ploughlands in the manor	Included in some cases when it is judged that there is potential for more arable
6	Hides in lordship	Sometimes not stated; usually because there was no in-hand land in that manor
7	Ploughs or ploughlands in lordship	Sometimes not stated; perhaps because there was no in-hand land in that manor
8	Villagers categorised in social class	But not identified by name or by what land they held individually or how much each held. It is suggested that all those listed were farming land and that is why they are listed. There is usually no indication of what labour obligations they owed to the lord of the manor
9	Ploughs or ploughlands with the villagers	The number of ploughs or ploughlands they held as a group and not individually
10	Livestock	Livestock is listed in Little Domesday, ICC and the Exeter Book, but not in Great Domesday. The numbers and species are also captured for two dates in Little Domesday. Poultry are not listed. We might suppose this data was captured in the original surveys for Domesday
11	Meadow	Usually listed; sometimes in acres
12	Woodland	When applicable; either measured in a capacity to graze pigs or in dimensions in leagues or furlongs. There is no indication of the type of woodland. The value of the timber is not recorded. Not all manors have woodland
13	Pasture	Not always listed. But in Nottinghamshire there is only one figure in each vill and recorded as 'woodland pasture'
14	Watermills	If applicable. Not every vill had a watermill or access to one. Domesday records rights in mills or millstones and not the mill building (Keith 2017)
15	The value of watermill	The separate value of the milling right is recorded in Great Domesday, and ICC but not Little Domesday. The mill values where recorded are probably not included in vill total
16	Fisheries	Only occasionally mentioned and may apply to rivers and fishponds rather than sea fishing
17	Value TRE	Usually included
18	Value when acquired	Not always included
19	VALUE 1086	This is the intended end result. Almost always recorded, but there are a few exceptions

TABLE 6 (opposite). Structure of typical Domesday entry for each manor

3.7 No hidden evidence

The data gathered were so comprehensive in relation to the agrarian detail that we might reasonably conclude that the listed assets included all those that were used to calculate the assessments. The valuations did not take account of some other assets, such as farm buildings, that were not listed and therefore cannot be seen by us now in the survey. However, the surveyors must have made judgements on the quality of the assets listed; the quality of the soil being perhaps the most important. Their judgements about quality are not visible to us now and thus any multiple regression, or other analysis, such as those carried out by McDonald and Snook (1985; 1986) cannot be completely successful.

3.8 Summary of procedures

We can draw six broad conclusions from a reading of Domesday:

1. The taxable unit is the manor situated in a specific vill; and this is the same taxable unit, or very similar, to that used for the Hidage assessments.
2. The taxpayer is the person in beneficial occupation of the manor, just as it was for the Hidage system. There is a clear continuity, although Domesday would have had to update the list of taxpayers.
3. As has been established, the essential targets of the survey were the mainly agrarian assets. The evidence from the survey is clear. As shown in Table 6, it is clearly a list of mainly agrarian assets. The boroughs are different.
4. There are also listed in a minority of vills: watermills, saltworks (not shown in Table 6), fisheries and occasionally churches, none of which are directly agrarian. They are recorded incidentally and randomly. Nevertheless, it is an agrarian list.
5. It was the land only that was assessed. This is what the survey clearly lists and describes in considerable detail. Again, the evidence of the survey is clear; other matters, such as livestock, are incidental. It is option 4.1 in Table 5.
6. The entries follow clear, tight and exact instructions in the order specified. If the surveyors had been meant to take into account other assets when making their valuations, these assets would have been specified in the terms of reference and the instructions and we would see the results recorded in the survey. The data collected is sufficient for valuation purposes although the surveyors would have made judgements on the quality of the assets.
7. By far the single most important item of data newly captured for the Domesday survey is the number of ploughlands. It is the pivot of the Domesday survey process as shown in Figure 2. This three-step process, from hides to ploughlands to rental value, is the central path; and this underlying structure is fundamental to the understanding of Domesday. Other listed assets influence, to a greater or lesser extent, the flow of the calculations from ploughlands to monetary assessment and affect the quantum of the 1086 valuation. Figure 2 shows the essential three elements.

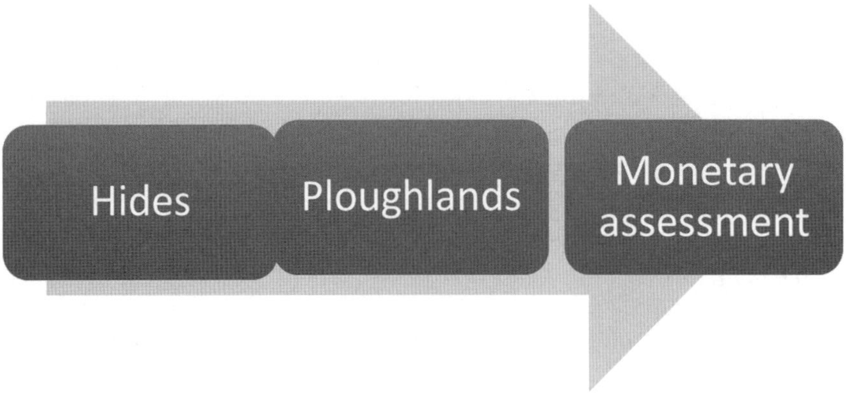

FIGURE 2 The basic structure

3.9 Hides and ploughlands

It is argued here that the Domesday survey follows on from the Hidage system and the concept of a ploughland was identical, or at least little different, to that of a hide. This line of reasoning has been identified by others, particularly Maitland (1989). But this is not recognised or accepted universally. It is an issue that is essential and important to the central structure of Domesday (see Maitland 1989 and also Holt in the introduction to that reprint). There four reasons to suppose that the concept of the hide was very similar to that of the ploughland in Domesday.

i) There are a few Hundreds in which the number of hides is exactly the same as the number of ploughlands (see Staploe in Table 7). There are other areas where there is a consistent ratio. These are statistically unlikely to be purely chance.

ii) In general the number of ploughlands exceeds the number of hides although the increase shows no obvious pattern. This is a result that could be expected from a revaluation after more than a century.[8] More land would have been cleared for arable over the years (Fig. 3).

iii) For most Hundreds there is a good correlation of hides to actual ploughlands. In Armingford, for all manors the correlation is 0.95. In Toseland it is 0.82. A random sample of 28 manors drawn from Great Domesday, which gave a correlation 0.92, suggests that Armingford and Toseland are not untypical. However, the Cornish correlations are less good but still above 0.75. The entries in Little Domesday are less easy to calculate because one or other of the figures is missing in a minority of the manors. However, the correlation for the Clavering half Hundred is 0.97, if two manors without a stated number of ploughs are excluded from the calculations. From a random and restricted sample of 21 entries for all Essex the correlation is 0.88.

---

8   For instance, for Armingford there are 109 hides and 162 actual ploughs. For Toseland the figures are 214 hides to 227 actual ploughs.

TABLE 7. Six Cambridgeshire hundreds with reduced hides

Hundred	Hides: original number	Hides: revised number	Plough-teams (rounded)
Staploe	90	50 or 60	90
Cheveley	50	29	84
Armingford	100	80	166
Longstowe	100	Difficult to count	137
Papworth	85	Difficult to count	121
Northstow	86	Difficult to count	83

FIGURE 3 Oxen ploughing (British Library Cotton MS Tiberius B V/1)

iv) If the concept of a ploughland for Domesday had introduced an entirely new basis, the introduction would have taken years to implement. The three timetables shown in Chapter 6 below would not have been feasible.

There are some caveats. The format of the survey, both in the way the data were collected and how they were finally recorded, gives a false impression of countrywide consistency. It is likely that there were many local agricultural methods, customs, and ways of holding and occupying land. The Domesday survey succeeds in forcing these local variations into a single, almost consistent, national format. It is because so much is recorded – and in such detail – that it is easy to suppose that the Domesday survey records everything and that it is more comprehensive than is, in fact, the case. What is not recorded in the Domesday Book is just as significant as what is. The following almost contemporary comment, in translation, by Robert, Bishop of Hereford provides an interesting, but not necessarily accurate, insight into the Domesday survey.

[In] the twentieth year of his reign, by order of William, king of the English, there was made a survey (description) of the whole of England, that is to say, of the lands of several provinces of England, and the possessions of each and all the magnate. This was done in respect of plough land and habitations, and of men both bond and free, both those who dwelt in cottages and those who had houses and some arable land and in respect of ploughs and horses and other animals; and in respect of services and payments due from all men in the whole land. Other investigators (inquisitors) followed the first; and men were sent into provinces which they did not know, and where they were themselves unknown, in order that they might be given the opportunity of checking the first survey, and, if necessary, of denouncing its authors as guilty to the king. And the land was vexed with many calamities arising from the collection of the royal money. (Galbraith 1974, 23)

Some, like Galbraith, have put great emphasis on this extract but it is at least confusing if it is meant to apply to Domesday, which seems likely to be the case. Using only the evidence of the contents of the Domesday survey it is apparent that the comments are inaccurate (or at least misleading in translation).

- First, the comment by Bishop Robert is inaccurate, specifically in relation to habitations, houses and huts, because they are not directly routinely recorded. Any mention of buildings as for instance *domus* in Huntingdonshire (Morris 1975, 7.8) or halls, *halla* (abbreviation) or *aula* in Nottinghamshire (Morris 1977, 9.26, 9.50) are few and incidental. If buildings, or even the sites of buildings, were meant to be taken into account the number of them could have been listed as is done in the Boroughs.

> ### Box 3. Hides: a system in use
>
> There is sparsity of pre-Domesday evidence about how the Hidage assessment system operated in practice. Clearly it operated well because we know substantial gelds were levied over a long period. In any taxation system there are always strains and disruption particularly from those who think they are over-assessed. They might be over-assessed because the pattern of agriculture had changed in their manor or area or there might have been a poor harvest. It might also be that the survey is correcting anomalies or previous under-counting. There would also those who used their power and position to influence their assessment. The lack of written records mean we rarely see these frictions in operation.
>
> The recording of the reduction of hides in some Hundreds in Cambridgeshire gives us a rare glimpse of these pressures. The situation is complicated by the number of hides being reduced, possibly temporarily. As Table 7 shows, this was the case for six of the 16 Hundreds in Cambridgeshire. None of the other ten Hundreds in Cambridgeshire had their Hidage assessments reduced. Those that were reduced, perhaps temporarily, seem to be associated with areas where the glacial till, chalky Boulder Clay on plateaus, predominates. Reductions do not seem to have been made in Hundreds mainly associated with soils from Lower Chalk, Gault Clay or Oxford Clay. Perhaps the reductions related to reduced productivity on the Boulder Clay lands due to wet years. We can do no more than guess.

3. What does Domesday record?   39

- Secondly, it is misleading because it is not comprehensive in respect to men or to animals (see the analyses in Appendices B and C). Bishop Robert of Hereford specifically mentions horses but these are not fully recorded.
- Thirdly, there is no mention in the above comment of woodland, pasture or meadow, all of which were of economic importance and affected the value of the arable land.
- Fourthly, services are not directly or routinely mentioned in the survey.
- Fifthly it is confusing because it talks about the collections of Royal money, but there seems no evidence that Domesday was ever actually used as a tax base. Perhaps it is a reference to rents from the Royal demesne only?

Just because a written source is contemporary does not mean it must be accurate.

The comment by Bishop Robert on 'other investigators' following the first, makes complete organisational sense. As explored above constant supervision would have been needed not only for the prevention of evasion but primarily to ensure national consistency. However, it would be impractical to repeat all the steps of the first survey. We might guess a selection of vills were visited either at random or where intelligence suggested impropriety. It is hard to see how the second investigators could have checked anything at all without actually visiting the vills.

3.10 What was omitted from the survey?

The Domesday surveyors required precise instructions on what information they were to collect and, by implication, what information was *not* required. Domesday contains a large amount of data and this analysis supposes that the survey collected the factual information that was required to complete the task. There is other information recorded randomly, unsystematically and incidentally from which we learn little directly relevant to Domesday. The systematic omissions from the Domesday list were important for those involved. They are important when calculating the logistics. It saves time if certain classes of land-related items do not have to be recorded. They are also important for historians using Domesday as a means of interpreting 11th century society. It is not a complete reflection of the economy or society. The Domesday omissions are worth noting because this emphasises the matters actually recorded. As in art, understanding and defining the negative space better describes the object.

3.11 No dwelling houses

To a modern valuer's eye the most striking omission relates to dwelling houses because almost none is listed in the survey outside the Boroughs. In a modern universal *ad valorem* valuation list (that is, one including all types of real property) prepared for annual or periodic property tax in any country in the World, the largest single class of entries, in both numbers and values, is always that of dwelling houses. Normally at least 80% of the entries relate to dwelling houses.[9] The total values of the dwelling houses and other buildings in any estimate of the total capital value of a country tend to amount to about half.[10] The proportions are much the same whether the list is prepared on the basis of annual rental values or capital values. This is now also the case both in developed economies and in less developed economies, such as those in Africa, and every country in which the writer has had professional experience. It was also the case in 1910 in the UK.[11]

Some commentators are of the opinion that that the word *manerium*, or its abbreviation in Domesday, implies the presence of a manor house (Loyn 1962). There are no dwelling houses specifically and directly recorded in Domesday outside the Boroughs. Even the manor houses directly related to the manors are not recorded and there must have been many of them. However, it probably would not be the case that every manor recorded in Domesday had a manor house. Dwelling houses would of course have existed in 1086. People were not sleeping in ditches. Shelter and warmth rank highly in a hierarchy of human physiological needs, after air, food and drink (Maslow 1943). The need for shelter is particularly important in latitudes 50° north (e.g. the UK) and therefore dwellings have a significant value. Some domestic houses might have been of impermanent construction and hardly worth recording, but many other houses must have been more substantial and would certainly have been of high value (see Appendix F). It might be that there were in number more than 300,000 dwellings in the area covered by the survey (see discussion of the size of the agricultural workforce in Appendix B). If those estimates are anywhere near correct there could not be less than 300,000 dwellings, not including those in the boroughs. The boroughs, including London and the other missing boroughs, might add another 60,000–80,000 dwellings and other buildings, in which case there were on average 15–20 houses in most average rural vills but these are invisible to us in Domesday. They are not routinely recorded there. When they appear they are merely incidental to other matters. If the structure of the manor houses or other buildings were part of the valuations, the variable type and constructional status of them would have been mentioned and classified

---

9 This figure probably includes buildings used partly as dwellings and, as often is the case in many developing countries now, partly also for commercial purposes.

10 Some indication of the proportions of value can be found in the UK Balance Sheet Estimates (ONS 2019).

11 The annual value of lands, houses etc, extracted from the Inland Revenue returns for 1910/11 relating to Income Tax Schedule A are as follows: Agricultural Land, including the farm buildings thereon £52 million, Houses and other buildings £222 million with £1 million for other rights (Whittaker 1914). Therefore, agricultural land, including the buildings thereon, only represented 20% of the total value. This was of course after the industrial revolution and the relative importance of agriculture was already less than it would have been in previous ages.

in Domesday because it would strongly affect the value of each house and then the total 1086 value of the manor. It would have required a considerable administrative undertaking.

The same applies in relation to ecclesiastical establishments. Although monasteries often had extensive agricultural enterprises, most of monastic life took place under cover in the monastery buildings. Monastery buildings are not recorded in the survey although some, we might guess, were substantial and valuable. The omission of dwelling houses, even manor and farmhouses, should not be surprising because, as many have pointed out, Domesday is clearly a record of the agrarian potential only. It was the agriculture and particularly the arable land that produced the surplus which supported other parts of the economy and which would have been the most readily taxable source. It means that Domesday excludes from a notional universal tax base perhaps about half of the potential national rental value.

3.12 No agricultural buildings

There must also have been many agricultural buildings, such as barns, granaries, dairies, cowsheds, stables, cart-sheds and stores. It would have been impossible to farm the land and produce and store seed corn and the surplus of other products without any buildings (see comments about farm buildings in Appendix A). The number and quality of these buildings would normally have been relevant to the agrarian potential and therefore would have influenced the value of the agricultural holding. The agricultural buildings are not recorded in the survey and there seems to be no evidence that they influenced the valuations.

3.13 No other buildings

Looking more widely, there are no buildings of any sort routinely recorded in Domesday except churches[12] in some counties and watermills when milling rights existed in that manor.[13] Such non-agricultural buildings would also have been in existence outside the Boroughs and included such as workshops, stores, shops, farriers/blacksmiths, tanneries, potteries, maltings, wheelwrights, horse and donkey mills and many others. Some of these buildings would certainly

---

12   There are 2016 churches recorded unevenly in Domesday. (Darby 1977, 346). The greater part of them, 65%, are in six counties. Suffolk has 427; Leicestershire has one. Fewer than 10% of the manors have churches listed. Some have land recorded with them and this could affect the 1086 value. The reason why others are included is unclear.

13   Mills are an exception only because they are specifically mentioned in the instructions. There must have been a reason for this which about which we can only guess. It could be that Domesday reference to mills relates to the millstones and/or the water power and the mill leats supplying it rather than the whole mill building. The mill value probably related to the monopoly value of the net revenue (Keith 2017).

have had significant values. They are not recorded in the survey; they are not included in the Domesday totals either and clearly were never intended to be included.

3.14 Recording other supporting agricultural assets

If, in Domesday, the main means of comparison, and the unit of valuation, is the plough- team, why were other assets recorded? The writer's view is that almost all the other items captured in the survey influence the productive capacity of the manor and the valuation of the arable land. They are the facts that an agricultural valuer would want to know. Manpower and the availability of agricultural labour is an important constraint (but see Appendix B which demonstrates that not all the agricultural manpower was always recorded in the survey). The availability or scarcity of grazing, particularly for the numerous draft oxen, would affect the farming and therefore the value of the arable land. Meadow would be of great importance for the supply of winter fodder. For a calculation of land usage see Appendix C.

3.15 Non-agricultural assets

There are some exceptions to the format described above and some rural assets recorded in the survey do not exactly fit the pattern outlined. Watermills, salt-pans and fisheries are recorded but are not primarily agricultural and do not directly influence the value of the arable land. However, all three have some strong relation to the land. The mills processed the grain and added value to it. The saltpans required wood to boil off the brine and therefore woodland was needed.

Mills are exceptional because they are the only asset class for which separate values are recorded, although this is not so in Little Domesday. In the writer's opinion, it is only river-fed watermills that are recorded in the survey. Tide mills almost certainly existed, particularly in Devon and Cornwall, just as they did in Ireland from at least the 7th century (McErlean and Crothers 2007). It is hard to find any Domesday mill recorded in parishes/vills where later tide mills were known to have existed (Minchinton 1977; Keith 2018). Horse and donkey mills must have existed in considerable numbers but generally do not seem to have been recorded.

There is no evidence that the Domesday surveyors sought to capture the value of quarries, clay pits or any other extractive enterprises. Building stone is rare in the eastern counties area studied, with the exceptions being sandstone from the Lower Greensand and the clunch from the shallow Totternhoe and Melbourn beds in the lower beds of the Chalk. They would no doubt have been extracting gravel and sand and chalk, and these quarries would have had a value. The survey does not concern itself with such mineral assets.

3.16 Resulting restricted tax base

Domesday is not a record of the built environment. The consequences of not including any buildings in the tax base might be that the Domesday value totals represent no more than half of the annual values of the notional national rental value of the entire 1086 real estate. However, the restricted tax base matters little if the purpose was to apportion the tax burden. No doubt the omitted assets would have been much more difficult to value and it would have been even more difficult, and perhaps impossible, to extract taxable money from them. This may be the reason Domesday, sensibly, focuses on agrarian assets which had well-known monetary values.

3.17 Identifying the underlying philosophy

Why were buildings, particularly agricultural buildings, omitted? In a society that was sophisticated enough to wage wars on a considerable scale, to move large armies across the seas, to organise and produce the Domesday Book, and to produce all the often sophisticated artefacts of the 11th century, suitable buildings were required and must, of course, have existed. There are several possibilities to consider. Could it be that all the buildings were too impermanent and had no value? It would seem that many Anglo-Saxon buildings were constructed predominantly of wood and other perishable materials such as small diameter timbers, wattle and daub, and cob walls all under a straw thatch or reed or shingle roofs, and mud floors. All such materials would have been particularly susceptible to decay, have a limited life, and limited physical remains would survive. Few of the buildings were of stone in the main study areas. None was of brick and tile after the Roman period until brick re-emerged in building materials in England well after 1086. Nevertheless, there would then have been many substantial and valuable buildings supporting a settled, long-established and complex civilisation which could, in theory at least, have been assessable for tax if required and would have added significantly to the tax base if that had been the intention. In practice it would have been much more difficult to assess and value buildings.

There already existed a tax on houses: the Papal tax known as 'Peter's Pence'. Could it be that the values of houses were excluded to avoid double taxation? However, there was already double taxation to some extent on agricultural land in that farmers and agricultural landowners paid tithe to the church in addition to any payments levied in relation to Hidage. The avoidance of double taxation does not seem likely. Furthermore, this does not explain why buildings other than dwellings were excluded.

It might be supposed that the Domesday survey simply continued the practice of the Hidage system, which seems to relate only to the value of the arable land. However, the Domesday survey was apparently more comprehensive in the data collected than might be the case for the Hidage assessment system, although both mainly relate to the arable land. In theory, it might have been technically possible to include at least the agricultural buildings if that had been desired, although this task would have taken several years; even perhaps decades. In practice, this might not have been a viable fiscal option.

A more probable scenario is that, under the law or custom, the ownership and thus the value of the improvements made on the land, such as the marking of boundaries, erection of buildings, planting of fruit trees, establishing and maintaining underwood, and the planting of growing crops which were carried out by the tenant, normally belonged to the tenant and not to a superior landlord. In which case, the King granted the land and the tenants-in-chief erected houses or, when applicable, monasteries and monastic buildings, farm buildings and made such developments and improvements to the land as were required to occupy and gainfully farm the land. It would then be the responsibility of the tenant-in-chief to maintain these improvements. If this was the case, the improvements might be thought to belong to the occupier who installed them and he/she should not pay rent on the added value they themselves had attached to the holding. Perhaps this practice went down the tenancy line to the sub-tenants. If such was the established law or custom, it might have been so well known that it was not necessary to state it in the terms of reference (which, in any case, we do not have). It would then accord with Ricardo's description made 700 years later in another context: 'Rent is that portion of the produce of the earth, which is paid to the landlord for the use of the original and indestructible powers of the soil' (1971, 91).

This last scenario seems to reflect the likely underlying philosophy. It was the most simple and practical course of action. It also fits the evidence of the survey. It is the writer's preferred scenario.

Box 4. Land value taxation

The absence of recording of buildings in Domesday is evidence of this being a survey of the land only as a basis for tax, albeit only of agricultural land. Then the Domesday survey and the gelds levied under Hidage assessment system are examples in practice of land based *ad valorem* property tax systems; sometimes called 'Site Value Rating' in the UK. This preceded by 800 years the writings and theory of Henry George on this subject (George 1881). His site value property tax theory also caught the attention of Ricardo, Malthus, Tolstoy, George Bernard Shaw and many others in the 19th and 20th centuries. Although his 'single tax' concept is clearly no longer viable, his underlying philosophy still has its adherents.

3.18 Woodland

The hypothesis put forward is that there is no assessed value included in Domesday that relates to the value of the standing timber (rather than underwood), or the value of the amenity or hunting potential of the woodland. The only value considered in the survey is that by which the woodlands supported and enhanced the usefulness of agriculture in that manor and, indirectly, the value of the arable land.

The value of woodland in more recent centuries, and probably before, usually depends on three main factors:

- the amount and quality of the standing timber, and
- the ease or otherwise of extraction and the proximity to markets, and/or
- the amenity and/or sporting value of the woodland.

The volume and quality of the growing timber normally makes a considerable difference to the value of the woodland and may often be the main determinate of value.[14] This is so at least for woodland with mature timber trees or trees that will grow into marketable timber. Areas of immature woodland present other valuation problems. This is so now and was no doubt the case in 1086. However, the value of standing timber is always difficult to tax.

Now, and during the last 60 years (at least), underwood and trees that are only useful for firewood have little value as standing timber because the cost of the labour of felling, cutting and extraction may well equal or exceed the sale price (although the demand for bio-mass is changing this situation in some circumstances). There has been almost no demand for coppicing for at least a hundred years, so coppice woodland has now no timber value, although the individual standard timber trees within the coppice area may have a value. There is now no general demand for woodland grazing. The circumstances in 1086 were different. In medieval times, it is supposed that there were many more uses for a wide range of woodland products which were essential for the life of the community and agriculture. Timber and underwood were no doubt traded because several vills in Cambridgeshire have little or no woodland recorded in Domesday but the inhabitants would have required wood products. Examples of manors without recorded woodland can be found in many counties.

---

14 From at least the year 1736, until the comparatively recent times (the 1970s), when the use of the metric measure commenced in the UK, timber has been of sufficient economic importance to have its own unique unit of measure of volume known as the 'hoppus' foot used in the British Isles and the British Empire. This reflects the worth placed on timber. Mixed woodland with valuable timber was (and to some extent still is) valued by measuring or estimating the timber volume of every tree of significant value. The formula was: Hoppus Volume (h ft) = ('Quarter Girth' (in))^2 × Length (ft)/144 = (circumference (ft)/4)^2 × Length (ft). It had the pre-electronic calculator advantage that it does not require the use of pi.

Coppicing of several tree species[15] for a number of purposes, including fencing material, agricultural and other tools, charcoal burning and domestic fuel, must have been central to the rural economy. These woodland uses are reflected in the legal names of ancient easements and profits-a-prendre such as 'estovers', 'bote' and 'pannage'. There are many references in Domesday to woodland providing fencing material.

There are only a few exceptions that do not support this general thesis with references to the use of woodland to supply material for houses, for instance in Hatley St George in Cambridgeshire (Morris 1981, 32.24). However, the houses to which this referred might be for those employed in agriculture and tied to the land. There is also a single reference in Huntingdonshire to timber for a specific large building in Whittlesey Mere (Morris 1975, 7.8).

In the 11th century woodland was clearly used for grazing and, particularly, for foraging pigs. Woodland grazing is no longer the norm although there are rewilding enterprises occurring. When compared with grassland grazing, hay and silage we have much less available scientific information about the quantity and quality of the nutrition supplied by tree leaves, the most useful species of tree or the seasonal variations in the quality of grazing and browsing. The Huntingdonshire Domesday tends to refer to woodland for grazing. In the Cambridgeshire survey there are frequent references to woodland as grazing for pigs with the number of pigs specified. In the half Hundred of Clavering, woodland is measured entirely by its potential capacity for grazing pigs, although this might by then have developed into a formal way of assessing the taxable size of the woodland.[16] The actual number of pigs in the Clavering half Hundred vills is recorded separately and the numbers do not match. Thus, there is stated to be woodland for 1300 pigs but only 210 pigs are actually recorded (both figures are the writer's count). All those factors, such as woodland grazing, coppicing, wood for fencing and firewood from fallen branches, can be seen as attributes supporting the agriculture of the manor or vill directly or indirectly. Simplicity is probably why the woodland is often measured by its grazing capacity.[17] However woodland had many other uses for the medieval farmer. An adequate

---

15 In Cambridgeshire, Huntingdonshire and north Essex, the evidence derived from large areas of derelict coppice woodland is that the species mainly coppiced there (at least in the last 300 years) was hazel, with ash being the second most common. Hazel coppice was often grown on a 7-year rotation. Ash coppice rotation might be about 20 years.

16 The Domesday surveyors must have had some formula in their minds that related the number of notional pigs to the area of woodland they were assessing. Rackham does not attempt to estimate any such formula perhaps because, as he correctly notes, woodland can vary considerably in its grazing carrying capacity (Rackham 1986, 75).

17 The distinction between pasture and woodland may not always have been clear on the ground. There were probably timber trees in or on the edge of many pasture fields. There may have been some managed woodland-pasture with trees cropped

area of woodland to support the agriculture of that manor would tend to add to the 1086 value. A lack of woodland would detract from that rental value.

In Cornwall and several other counties the woodland is measured in dimensions of leagues (see Appendix F). It is possible to calculate an approximate area of the woodland. However, this does not indicate the use or quality of the woodland. The value could vary considerably depending on whether it was underwood/coppice, mature forest or only unmanaged immature woodland, or many variations of these. If the mature timber value of the woodland was to be reflected there would have to be more detail recorded than we see in Domesday.

In Nottinghamshire the survey generally records only 'woodland pasture' (*silua past*)[18] making no distinction between the two (although meadow is recorded separately and sparsely). We might speculate that there are several possible reasons for this. Maybe it simply accorded with local custom. More likely it reflected the systematic devastation of the landscape caused by the 'harrying of the north' in 1070 following the English/Danish rebellion; and that afterwards the care and management of pasture and woodland was absent or degraded with much being used only for rough grazing (Bates 2016, 313). Maybe it reflected reality and it was often difficult to define exactly what was woodland and what was pasture.

In addition to the usage of woodland to support agriculture there would have been the value of the standing timber, particularly those species of trees large enough in girth and length to have a potential for structural use. Long, large diameter, sound, well-grown trees of species that can be used for structural and other purposes are rarer and therefore more valuable. They take a long time to grow and a long time to replace when felled. The value is determined by the volume and quality and species of the standing timber. This is the case now and it must have always been so although demand may fluctuate.[19] There would certainly have been some large, valuable, individual timber trees and stands of timber trees in some of the woods (at least in some vills/parishes and in some hedgerows) and these would have had a significant value.[20] There is no evidence in Cambridgeshire, Huntingdonshire or the Essex half Hundred of Clavering of these timber values being included in the Domesday totals. This appears to be the case in other parts of the country. In contrast, coppice woods and osier

---

by pollarding and with usable managed pasture in between. There were no doubt rides and glades within the woodland that could be grazed.

18 The references probably do not mean that it was carefully managed 'woodland pasture' with pollarded trees set wide enough apart to create areas of managed pasture between.

19 The analyses of vernacular medieval timber buildings frequently shows that few large timbers were used and that much of the wood is from small diameter trees or branches. This might imply that there was always a shortage of large timbers.

20 The term 'timber' is used in a general sense. In Common Law, *timber* referred only to the species oak, ash and elm.

beds were certainly then of value although measured and valued in a different way. We might guess that this value influenced the value of the manor.

We might suppose that the survey instructions did not require the surveyors to ascertain information relevant to the value of standing timber. Perhaps the standing timber did not always belong to the manor in which it was situated. The values of woodland for hunting and amenity purposes do not generally seem to have been included in the survey even in the Royal forests; such values would, in any case, have been difficult to assess and it would have been even more difficult to extract tax from them.

3.19 Summary of what is assessed

The Domesday survey is essentially a revaluation of an *ad valorem* property list. It does two things. It reviews the Hidage assessments and reassesses them as ploughlands. Although the underlying concept of the hide and ploughland were either identical or very similar, this step was necessary because all tax bases deteriorate over time for a number of reasons and need re-assessing. Domesday then re-values the ploughlands in monetary terms. It is not concerned with the built environment and does not systematically record it in Domesday.

The bases of assessment were as follows:

- The taxpayers are those holding from the King outside the Royal demesnes.
- The assessed assets were only those related to agriculture, except in the Boroughs. It is an agrarian valuation list. That was the purpose of the Domesday survey.
- The unit of assessment was the manor in each vill.
- The asset to be valued is the farmland only and not the buildings and improvements thereon.
- The unit of comparison and valuation was the arable land denoted as ploughlands.
- The underlying concept of a ploughland was the same as that for the hide.
- The value of the ploughlands was influenced by other supporting factors including, among other agrarian assets, the amount of meadow and pasture.
- Woodland was assessed only as an attribute to the agrarian value of the manor.

3.20 Rationale for focus on arable land

Domesday agriculture was certainly well above subsistence level. We can form some quite detailed impressions of medieval agriculture from other documents (see Appendix A). We can be certain that agriculture generated sufficient surpluses to pay rents and it might be supposed that these agricultural revenues were the mainstay of the 1086 economy. We cannot know from Domesday alone how the levels of the rents related to agricultural outputs. Therefore, we do not know from reading Domesday alone what the level of rents might have been in relation to other things in the economy. Nor do we know how affordable or exploitive were agricultural rents in 1086.

There is not much information in Domesday about the outputs of pastoral agriculture, although the numbers of animals listed in Little Domesday and ICC give some indication of stocking rates. No doubt such livestock outputs, such as meat, dairy products, hides and wool, were a significant part of the economy, even in the now more arable eastern counties. In those counties with large areas of unploughable land, these outputs must have been more important (see Appendix F comparisons with Cornwall). Why then does Domesday focus on arable land? Why is the arable land the means of comparison? It is generally agreed that the arable land provided in the form of grain, the main saleable, exchangeable and portable commodity, which was readily convertible to cash and comparable throughout the Domesday survey areas. Grain also has the longest storage life of all the usual agricultural products. Furthermore, grain, and the milled outputs from it, would have been needed to supply the army. Perhaps this is why mills were included with separate assessments. The outputs from the pastoral land, although having ascertainable market prices, would have had fewer of these qualities. No doubt cereal products were the main staple of the diet but we might suppose that there were wide array of other foodstuffs available such as vegetables, fruits, honey, nuts, eggs, poultry and fish, at least to those who could afford them. These are hardly visible in Domesday and were probably produced in gardens and small plots, particularly in locations readily accessible to markets. The arable land therefore provided a measure of ability to pay and probably the best one available. Once again it was the most practical fiscal solution.

3.21 The hide

The recording of the existing Hidage assessments was the central starting point for almost every Domesday entry. It is important to attempt to understand (as far as is possible) the concept of the hide, which was certainly ancient by 1086. It was well known in the 8th century and is mentioned in 11 locations in *The Ecclesiastical History of the English People* by Bede in AD 731. Six listings are shown in Table 8 as in translation (Farmer and Sherley Price 1990).

It is clear – even from these few references – that the land measure of the hide was not nationally consistent in superficial area. See column G in Table 8 and note the percentages that are more than 100%, which would be impossible if the hide was universally 120 acres. There are references to five islands in Bede: Thanet, Anglesey, Isle of Man, Iona and Isle of Wight (Fig. 4). We know the superficial areas of them as now calculated (marine erosion over a thousand years would have had little effect on the figures). From this, we can calculate that, for Thanet and for the Isle of Wight, the area of a hide as estimated for these islands must have been markedly less than 120 acres (this applies even if the area of medieval Thanet is understated in Table 8). The analysis rests on

Page ref in Farmer & Sherley-Price 1990	Location	Hides according to Bede	Area of hides in acres as if 120 per hide	Modern measure in km²	Modern acreage	Area in hides* as % of the modern acreage	Comments
A	B	C	D	E	F	G	H
75	Thanet	600	72,000	103	25,452	283	Perhaps the hide measure was markedly smaller in this region. However, there must be some doubt about whether the total area is correct as Thanet is not now a sea-girt island
118	Anglesey	960	115,200	714	176,358	65	The figures are as might be expected for 120 acre hide
118	Isle of Man	300	36,000	572	141,284	25	Some of the island is mountainous and not suitable for hidation. The hides might have been 120 acres
148	Iona	5	600	9	2174	28	
225	Sussex	7,000	840,000	1,991	491,777	171	Either the hide measure was smaller in this region or the Bede reference does not correspond with modern Sussex
231	Isle of Wight	1200	144,000	380	93,860	153	The hide measure must have been smaller on this island

*Taken here to be 120 acres, see text

the assumptions that: i) the normal mean size of a hide was then about 120 acres (which is as shown a debatable assumption) and ii) Bede's recording of the hide numbers are approximately accurate. Clearly his figures were rounded.[21] The manner in which Bede refers to the hides suggests that the hide – as a land measure – was well established by the 8th century. It is tempting to try to relate the hide to the Roman *Centuria* which were (usually) 200 *Jugeria* or about 125 acres (51 ha). However, this was only one of at least three multiples of the *Jugerium* and the approximate numerical coincidence proves nothing. We might guess that the Hidage assessments were already by then a basis for a quota tax, as they were known to be by the 10th century, for the collection of Danegeld. Otherwise, how would Bede have known these figures?

Over a century ago, in the first edition dated 1897, Maitland said: 'What was the Hide? However unwilling we may be to face this dreary old question,

---

[21] It has been pointed out that: 'if the numbers in Col C are regarded as households, then the gross acres per household are as follows. Thanet:42 {corrected figure} acres, Anglesey 183 ac, I o M 470 ac, Iona 434 ac, Sussex 70 ac, I o W 78 ac. In terms of the carrying capacity of the different landscapes, these relativities are a pretty good fit.' (Alec Tompson in private correspondence 6/2020).

3. *What does Domesday record?* 51

TABLE 8 (opposite).
Bede: Some references
to the hide (Farmer and
Sherley-Price 1990)

FIGURE 4 Six hidage assessments in Bede as shown in Table 8

we cannot escape it' (Maitland 1989, 357). To a surveyor with an interest in land measurement, valuation and property taxes, the question is not dreary. It is central to the complete understanding of the Hidage assessments and then, consequently, to understanding Domesday itself. Unfortunately, we may never have this complete understanding. Without doubt, the Domesday surveyors and their precursors would have had a clear and precise notion of what was the concept of a hide. Clarity would have been essential to the use of the hide as a land measure as a basis for calculation of rent and, probably less often, for capital sums on sale and, when necessary, for taxation. The definition of the hide would tend to have become more precise locally in concept over the period of at least two centuries, although there clearly was a lack of national consistency. We might guess that this lack of national consistency was something that Domesday was intended to correct. Can we know what was meant by a hide? This path to identify the hide has been very well travelled, particularly by 19th century scholars. It leads us through such terms *terra unius familiae, terra unius manentis, hiwisc, hiwscipe*, and *hid* (Maitland 1989, 358 *et seq.*). Greirson says 'The hide (OE. hid) was notionally the extent of land that would support a household' (Grierson 2003, 121).

The description of a hide as the extent of land to support a household or family generates many questions. Clearly it does not apply to the labour applied to the agriculture and the cultivation of a hide. As shown in Appendix B, agriculture in medieval times must have required, approximately at least, one adult male (or the equivalent in female and child labour) per 10 acres of farmed land. Thus, a single hide required the labour of at least a dozen men. This is more than the average family would provide. It is also much larger than we might suppose an average agricultural unit would be at that time. Many centuries later, in 1851, more than 60% of the holdings were under 100 acres and about 40% below 50 acres (Grigg 2019). These holdings were in any case supporting more than one family when different generations and hired labour are taken into account. If we had comparable figures for 1086 we might guess that the agricultural family holdings were much smaller than those in 1851. Perhaps the average peasant was supporting himself and family on a 15-acre virgate. Most farmers before the mid-20th century were supporting themselves and their families on fewer than 100 lowland acres.[22] If a 120-acre hide is too large for the labour of a single family unit (if that is what is meant by *familiae*)

---

22 Mean farm sizes in England now and in at least the last 200 years tend to be larger than those in continental Europe and much larger than those in most parts of South-east Asia and in many other parts of the world. In the post-war former Yugoslavia a maximum size of agricultural holding was specified in law as 10 ha (24 acres) per person. In Guyana in the 1960s and 1970s irrigated two crop per year rice fields were leased by the state in units of 4 or 8 acres. Although in neither case did the prohibitions completely succeed, in attempting to restrict the occupation of larger areas they illustrate that 120 acres would be considered a very large farm in many parts of the world.

and much larger than most farmers could aspire to during the next 900 years, then what exactly was meant by a household? Disappointingly, this line of enquiry takes us no nearer any precise definition of a hide than was achieved by the 19th century historians.

We can have more success through another line of inquiry. The hide as a measure was probably identical to, or little different from, the carucate or 'sulung' which are thought to be a measure of the amount of land a team of eight oxen could plough in a year; see for instance amongst others Grierson (2003, 122; see also Appendix C for comments on oxen ploughing). This makes sense. If the 3-field systems were as common in 1086 as the later evidence of pre-enclosure parishes tends to show, then we may suppose that a not unusual arrangement is a three crop rotation: a winter-sown crop (perhaps rye or wheat of some sort), followed by a spring-sown crop (perhaps barley or legumes), followed by fallow, and then repeating again with a winter-sown crop. The greater part of the ploughing would have occurred in the 3 months from mid-August to mid-November. In any one hide the 40-acre fallow would have to be ploughed, a seed-bed prepared and sown for next year's winter sown crop and the crop established during this period. The 40-acre winter-sown crop for this year would be harvested and, if possible, the land ploughed before winter conditions set in. The land would then be left in furrow over winter which allows the elements to aid the formation of a tilth which would help the creation of the seed bed for the spring-sown crop. The 11th century reeves and farmers would no doubt have known this. The 40-acre spring-sown crop would be harvested and the land left fallow.[23] Thus, 80 acres would be ploughed in about a 13-week period. Assuming a 6-day working week, this requires the ploughing of about an acre each working day. Oxen are slower than horses but, nevertheless, this is a demanding if feasible plan; easier to achieve on light land than on heavy. During this same period there would be 80 acres to harvest; a task requiring considerable manpower.[24] This might have been the aim but, of course, agricultural life is not that neat. Weather interferes. It is not possible to plough if the land is too wet. In some years of wet autumns the land for the next year's spring crop would have to be left as stubble over the winter and ploughed in the spring. This might, in any event, have been the local custom in some vills; and there are some advantages to spring ploughing. In other years, a dry, clement, winter might allow ploughing over that period. On the other hand, in many years there would be no ploughing possible during the winter months in, for instance, January, notwithstanding the 'Plough Monday/Sunday' Festival during that month. Whatever the arrangements, ploughing of 80 acres has to be done

---

23 It may be that the 3-field system was less common than the 2-field system at least in some regions. If so, the figures can be recalculated in that basis. It makes little difference to the broad conclusion.

24 The harvest of 80 acres probably required about 200 man/days for the weather-sensitive tasks of reaping and binding alone. In addition, there was the labour required for the immediate stooking, and later carting and putting into thatched ricks.

after autumn harvest and before spring sowing can start, and the winter weather restricts the opportunities. In spite of these uncertainties, the general concept of a hide or carucate or sulung being a measure that could be ploughed by a team of oxen in the year makes practical sense.

It is difficult, for us, to understand fully the concept of the hide and it might probably always be impossible. Nevertheless, it was a measure widely understood in the 11th century and before. It would seem very likely that it was related to carrying capacity of the agricultural land even if the measure was not nationally consistent. The measure of a hide needed little revision over the years since it did not date as a consequence of inflation. It was effective fiscally over more than a century and that is the crucial test. It was efficiently carried out nationally. It was thorough in its administration, as can be seen from the Hidage assessments recorded in Domesday. Of course, the tax base did deteriorate over time as circumstances changed. The important difference between hides and ploughlands is not one of fundamental concept but of time. Hides related to circumstances in the early 10th century or well before that. The ploughlands of Domesday relate to circumstances in about 1086. There were regional inconsistencies and omissions in the Hidage assessments. Nevertheless, the Hidage system of assessment and the effective collection of various gelds from this base were a professional fiscal triumph. Most of our knowledge about the hide at a local level comes from Domesday. The Domesday survey was built on these solid foundations.

CHAPTER 4

Valuation

4.1 Annual sums and not capital values

It has been established by many others – using a wide historical perspective – that the assessed figures in Domesday relate to annual sums. However, in accordance with the aim of this work we should not take this for granted and go back to basics. Even if we were to look only at the evidence of the survey itself, the figures could hardly be anything else. Capital values would have been less useful fiscally because, then as now, agricultural land rarely changed hands in arms-length transactions in the open market. Thus, sales evidence is harder to find and less consistent. In the UK in modern times, with a relatively active market, only about 1 ha in 10,000 is sold annually on the open market at arms-length. This situation is quite typical throughout the world although many agricultural land markets are markedly less active and most very much less transparent. This may well have been the case in England in the 11th century. However, land was then bought and sold (as Appendix F demonstrates) and it is possible to estimate the approximate level of the capital value of agricultural land. Nevertheless, the volume of evidence for the rental market would have been much larger, more reliable and a better indication of ability to pay.

4.2 What annual sums?

It is necessary to distinguish three different annual figures which might in theory be used as bases for assessment. They are:

i) total output,
ii) net output,
iii) rent or rental value.

The first theoretical option is the gross annual output, that is to say, the total value of the actual produce of the agricultural unit. In other words, this would be a basis for a turnover-like tax which would fix the geld payable as a fraction of that assessment, in, say, pence or shillings in the pound. This basis has not been suggested by any other commentator but, nevertheless, it is an option that should be examined.

Gross turnover is not a good measure of ability to pay, especially in years with adverse weather or when prices are low and when there is no surplus. It would also have been difficult – and sometimes impossible – to express the gross annual output in money terms. Nevertheless, this possibility cannot be dismissed out of hand because it was the underlying basis of the tithe for around 1000 years. One-tenth of the gross produce was an onerous burden. For the tithe, it initially applied to the actual production in that year and was paid in kind and assessed and collected at a local level. It was, of course, founded on a religious obligation. The subsequent history of the tithe with its legal complexities and the problems of commuting payments in kind to monetary payments do not suggest that it would have been easy – or even possible – to use an estimated value of the gross output for each manor. In any case, the data collected in the survey does not look as if it is designed to assist the surveyors in estimating the actual gross output. Nor does the wording suggest it. The Domesday survey, unlike the tithe, was not founded on a religious obligation. The tithe was assessed and collected locally, usually in kind. Furthermore, if such a measure were required it would be necessary to reassess each holding every year.

Another second option might, in theory, be a calculated estimate of the mean agricultural annual profit. This perhaps seems to been suggested by others. For instance, Harvey says: 'it was within the capacity of the great Domesday Inquiry to find out and record the expected annual returns from land at two or three crucial dates. It was within its capacity to estimate the full potential of land in cash terms, especially where land had been laid waste' (Harvey 2014, 206). It might be that this means the net profit rather than rental value. If so she under-estimates the difficulties. McDonald and Snook state that 'the capacity of a manor to pay tax can be measured in the terms of the value of its output as well as in terms of its resources' (1985, 369). If this means the total agricultural output or the net profit (before rent) rather than the rental or rental value, it is at least mis-leading. Neither description is exact. It is not clear that anyone has examined the practical difficulties in computing such sums, if they are not the rental values. Within this option there are again two possibilities. The first is the *actual* individual net profit of that *actual* holding for that year in a manner rather similar to an income tax. The second is a general estimated net revenue that might be gained from working land of similar character to that being assessed by a farmer with reasonable ability.

The first, an actual profit, is impractical because:

i) not many would not know the amount of the profit in money terms;
ii) outputs and profits would vary from year to year; and
iii) demesne income would have come from several sources, not all agrarian.

Furthermore, many manors would not actually make a profit on their in-hand land. There is also the problem of 'own consumption' which would mask the actual profit or real benefit. This factor has been correctly identified by Harvey (2014). Such an assessment of the actual profit would be similar to income tax and there are good reasons why income tax was not imposed in the UK until 1799. It still remains difficult to administer, particularly in developing economies. For instance, in Pakistan in 2016, with a population of about 193,000,000, the number of income taxpayers was fewer than 857,000. Impressive though the

of King William's regime clearly was, it would not have
lity to impose a tax similar to income tax. Furthermore,
d and taxation philosophy would have been different to
hich applies to individuals, rather than being attached to
g. If it were to be a credible tax, it too would have to be
It is not a feasible option.
, the net output or the average profit for that holding,
 assess because typical outputs and/or profitability in
 so many factors and vary from year to year, from farm
mer to farmer. Some of those commenting on Domes-
m to have appreciated the skills required in agriculture.
nts can starve in bad years. Soviet collective farms were
nprofitable. Farmers in the developed world can, and do
rupt. The practical difficulties of calculating and average
least complex and difficult. It is impractical. Why even
ise?
theoretically not completely impossible because this was
oleonic cadastres did in the early 19th century (see Textbox
ilarities in the agricultural data collected for Domesday
ed for the Napoleonic cadastres. Nevertheless, there are
ay was not like the Napoleonic cadastres and was not an
fitability. In summary the reasons are these:

rent underlying concept. The Napoleonic cadastre was
ntum tax while Domesday is clearly the basis for a quota

ot assessed plot by plot. The taxable unit was the manor,
se, both systems gathered the scattered holdings into the
ders/taxpayers.
not a practical method in 1086. By the early 1800s, there
dge of the science of agriculture and of crop yields and
ties.
would have taken years, if not decades; just as it did for
adastres.

- It would have been impossible for Domesday to impose a new system of taxation, that is to say, on the average net profit, without a long period of development. The Napoleonic cadastre had such a long development period. There is no evidence that Domesday had any suitable fiscal ancestors that would serve for a 'net profit' tax.

It seems to have been suggested that the net profit system applied only to the demesne land (McDonald and Snook 1986). Perhaps the reasons for this supposition might be that, as no rent was passing in those instances, no rental assessment could be made. If so, this supposition is entirely incorrect. This is no impediment to the calculation of a rental value. Valuers are doing so all the time.

There are other reasons to consider that the supposition about demesne land having values calculated in a different manner is incorrect. First, the practical difficulties for any non-rental assessment, as described above, remain whatever

> **Box 5. The Napoleonic Cadastre in France**
>
> No tax or land registration system comes into being suddenly without precedent. All reflect developments taking place over long periods (Cleargot 2003). The development of the Napoleonic cadastre certainly had a long and difficult development that started before the revolution. Its general aim was clear from an earlier declaration in 1804: *l'assiette de la contribution foncière sera répartie par égalité proportionnelle sur toutes les propriétés foncières à raison de leur revenu net* (The base of the land contribution will be distributed by proportional equality over all land properties at the rate of their net income).
>
> Notwithstanding those words, it was conceived as a quantum tax being fair and predictable unlike the previous quota taxes of the ancient regime, *taille réele* or *taille personnelle*. The new tax was to be fair, detailed and scientifically based. It was probably impossible to introduce such a radical concept until after the revolution. The technical challenges were considerable and it required Napoleon's strong administrative command to implement. Work did not start until a law of 1807. The enormous task was described in it as follows:
>
>> Measuring a stretch of more than seven thousand nine hundred and one square myriametres, over a hundred million plots; making a map for each commune showing these one hundred million plots; classifying all of them according to soil fertility; assessing taxable revenues on each one of them; gathering all the scattered plots belonging to the same owner under a single name and defining, by adding together all the different revenues, the total revenues of that person and recording those revenues, Official thenceforth the basis for tax assessment, such is the aim of this operation. (official translation from Cleargot 2003)
>
> It was map based and the basic unit was the individual plot. Initially, it was mainly concerned with agricultural land. The surveying technical expertise already existed in France and a large number of surveyors were required for the task, which stretched the national capacity. The plots were classified according to use – pasture, arable, orchard, vineyard, etc. It took 40 years and was never fully complete in France. Nevertheless, it was and is the foundation of the modern French cadastral system. Similar systems were adopted in many European countries, particularly those in the Austro/Hungarian Empire. Cadastres were also introduced earlier in some of the countries conquered by Napoleon. For instance, the cadastre for the Netherlands that took 26 years from 1806 (see Box 2). In both cases they had the advantage of large-scale, mainly 1:2500, up-to-date maps.

the tenure. Secondly, it should not be supposed that the in-hand demesne land necessarily made a profit. Many home farms on large agricultural estates in the UK in the second half of the 20th century ran at a loss, notwithstanding a favourable tax and subsidy system. Thirdly, it would not be practical to assess the demesne land using a different method to that for the let land because it is unlikely that the extent of the demesnes land remained stable over the years. Land would be let or taken in hand as circumstances required. Why apply different methods of assessment to the two categories? It would be an unnecessary complication.

The easiest and most obvious option is to follow the rental market for all manors, let or otherwise. Why should we suppose the Domesday values are anything else? The concept of leasing and annual rents was, and is, widely understood throughout the World, historically and geographically. There is no reason to suppose that this was not so in England in 1086. The assessed annual figures must relate to either rents or rental values in some form for both demesne lands and the let lands.

4.3 Rents and renting

The evidence of the Domesday survey provides a good guide to what was assessed and next we need to consider how it was assessed. The rack rent (the full open market rent) is some proportion of the net profit, which is available to both reward, or at least sustain, the farmer and be available for the payment of rent to the owner or superior landlord. The market will determine how this net profit is divided between landlord and tenant. It might be supposed that, in the 11th century, the peasant farmers had little negotiating leverage. Nevertheless, there is a limit to the amount a landlord can extract from a farmer. Farming is not an easy occupation and the landowners needed the skills and toil of the farmers if they were to receive a rental income.[1] There will also be poor years or poor periods when profitability is so bad that there is no net profit and no rent can be paid. This was so during the potato famines in the 1840s in both Ireland for 7 years and in Scotland over an 8-year period. The multiplication of grain (the increase in the proportion of the seed sown to that harvested) in arable farming must average in the long term more than about two to be sustainable

---

[1] The proportion of rent to gross agricultural output varies greatly. In a free market with a reasonable demand and without any statutory restrictions, rents might typically amount to between 10% and 20% of the gross output. In times of agricultural depression, such as the period before the Second World War in the UK, rents were close to zero. For many farmers, there was no surplus at that time. At the other extreme, in the Indus valley in Pakistan in the 1990s, peasant cultivators were not uncommonly farming land (mainly irrigated two crops a year rice but also a variety of other crops) with share-cropping arrangements in which the gross yield was shared 50% each between landowner and farmer (although in many cases the landowner supplied some of the capital and paid the taxes).

even before rent. We know that after marked improvements in agriculture in the 17th century, the multiplication rate for wheat could vary from factors of six to 14 (see Bowden 1990 and Appendix A). Perhaps typical multiplication rates were half this in the 11th century.[2] This leaves little surplus to protect the famer in a bad year, and still less with which to pay rent.

The *Anglo-Saxon Chronicle* also tells us that 1086 was a bad year:

> And in the same year there was a very heavy season, and a swinful and sorrowful year in England, in murrain of cattle, and corn and fruits at a stand, and so much untowardness in the weather, as man may not easily think: so tremendous was the thunder and lightning, that it killed and it continually grew worse and worse with men. (*Anglo-Saxon Chronicle,* for year 1086, Ingram and Giles 1847)

Using the restricted sources of this study, it is not clear whether this affected the assessments determined in Domesday.

4.4 Rental value or rent passing

The next issue to determine is whether the figures are rental values or actual rents passing (rents being paid). This is an important distinction. An examination of the Domesday text in the areas studied gives a clear indication that the assessments generally relate to rental values. The English translations in the Phillimore and Penguin editions use the words 'value' or 'worth'. The Latin as shown in Phillimore is, depending on tense or form and abbreviation, variously *Val* or *ualent* or *ual* or *valuit*. However, there is not complete consistency and the terms such as *redere*, in various tenses, are also used almost at random. Perhaps those terms were inserted when the actual rent passing was thought to represent a fair market rental value. If, on the other hand, the survey had been recording only actual rents passing, there would have been no reason to ever use terms relating to worth or valuation. The indications are therefore that the survey records assessed rental values in all cases.

This contrasts with the wording relating to the rents or other payment for dwellings, messuages or plots for dwellings in the boroughs in which the translated words 'worth' or 'value' are very rarely used. These references in the boroughs are clearly the sums passing (see Section 14.3 below for a discussion on the data captured in the Boroughs). Where assessments of mills are recorded in the manors, the abbreviated Latin uses neither forms of *valuere* or *redere*. Typically, the Latin entries record such words as *i. molin de x sol.* or *ii. molin de xvi, sol.* For the mills in the boroughs, the word *reddit* (or a shortening of it or in some other tense) is often used. It might therefore be supposed that, for mills, the survey records an actual rent passing. It would, in any case, be difficult to estimate the rental value of a mill because of the many variations in milling capacity (the rate of flow of the harnessed water and the head) and the

---

2   The comparable modern figure for the multiplication of seed for, say, winter wheat is about a factor of 40 in England.

monetary yield being dependent on a monopoly value and local demand. In such circumstances a modern rating valuer would typically resort to the little used 'profits valuation' method.

Domesday gives little indication of how and when rents were paid. Was there a nationwide norm?[3] This seems unlikely because, almost within living memory, there were customary regional variations for quarterly rent-days for farms. Were rents normally paid quarterly, half-yearly or yearly? Were rents paid in advance or in arrears? Such variations are of considerable importance to tenants and landowners and affect the amount of affordable rent. We might guess that, for national consistency, the Domesday value assessments made certain common assumptions and the rental value was calculated on this common basis, whatever the actual circumstances. There is no indication in Domesday what such assumptions might have been made.

4.5 *Ad firmam*

An added complication is that, in some instances, Domesday refers to the property being at farm – *ad firmam*[4] (see, for instance, Woodditton in Cambridgeshire; Morris 1981, 1.11); although the Phillimore editions always translate this term as 'at revenue'. It could be that this is simply another way of saying that it is rented. But it seems more likely that it then had a more specific meaning, just as it did in relation to taxation at later dates. Tax-farming had two essential characteristics. The first is that the payment for the farmed rights was paid in advance for a specific period. The advance payment was the important essential feature. The second is that the 'tax farmer' acquired certain defined rights to stand in the shoes of grantor. For taxes, the 'farmer' had the legal rights to assess and collect certain taxes for a certain period.[5] We might guess that Domesday references to manors *ad firmam* had both characteristics. Perhaps the price was paid in advance and, in return, the 'farmer' acquired certain rights for a defined period, and he took all the risks. It might be that the arrangements were a 'vif-gage'.[6] It might be that, in some cases, it was a simple lease for a term stated (in years or lives) with the full rent or a premium for the term paid in advance. All such measures would fill various specific

---

3   See the discussion of this topic by Welldon Finn (1961, 138). He is, however, discussing the payment of a geld rather than the norm for rent payments.
4   The question is further complicated by the old English term *feorm* for food rent. The two words might be related but have taken on different meanings over time.
5   In France, during the *Ancien Regime* in the 18th century before the revolution, probably more than half the Royal taxes were farmed and the tax-farmers supplied services to the state well beyond the mere collection of taxes. In England, the practice was rare, although the collection of the customs was farmed for a period from 1558 by Thomas Smythe. Tax farming was widely used in the British Empire.
6   A living pledge with the lender in possession, as distinguished from a mortgage (or dead pledge) with the borrower in possession.

needs in specific circumstances. It might be that these rights and obligations (whatever the legal form) often included all those that ran with the ownership of the manor, including those relating to soke and sake and including the use of the manor house (if any) and any other buildings and other non-agrarian profits. If so, the rights acquired for manors-at-farm were greater – and therefore more valuable – than those being assessed for taxation in Domesday or for the Hidage assessment, which related only to the bare agricultural land. It has been noted that the consideration for manors-at-farm can be higher than the average and this might be the explanation (see examples in Darby 1977, 211). On the other hand, revenues paid in advance should be less. A pound paid now is worth more than a pound to be paid in a year's time. Domesday (on its own) does not contain enough detail to do anything more than allow us to guess what is meant by *ad firmam*, but the writer's opinion is that it almost certainly did have a specific meaning.[7]

4.6 Actual or potential ploughlands

It should again be noted that Domesday is a record of agricultural land not the built environment. Generally it is not recording assets. Any record of assets, whether ploughs or the ploughs with the ox teams and the tack or livestock, is as an aid to assessing the value of the fiscal unit of land: here termed the 'ploughland'.

The next question is whether the Domesday surveyors were assessing for rental value the existing use value, as indicated by the actual number of ploughlands in the manor, or the potential value as the potential number of ploughlands that could be there. This only applies to a minority of manors in some counties where it is noted that there could be more arable. We might guess that this means cleared land not in use as arable. It seems unlikely that it meant woodland that could be assarted because clearing woodland, removing the roots and converting to arable, can take years.

The actual ploughlands referred to are those referred to in row 4 of Table 6, above. These two assessments mean, in property tax terms, the value of the holding as it stands (in Rating terms the Latin jargon is *rebus sic stantibus*) or, in the alternative, its *highest and best* use. In this case, both terms relate to the agrarian value only. In the first instance we might guess that the key valuation figure, where there are two figures, is the potential number of ploughlands in the manor because otherwise why collect this information? However, the limited evidence from Table 9 is not supportive of this thesis.

In Armingford the difference in the correlations of actual ploughlands to £s to potential ploughlands to £s is not significant. Nor is it if only the manors in Armingford with different figures for potential ploughlands to actual ploughs

---

[7] See Postan's remarks (1993, 107), although it may be that the importance of the advance payment of a rent or premium is not fully recognised.

TABLE 9. Correlations of ploughlands or hides to £s per plough

	Armingford in DB	Armingford in ICC	Toseland	Clavering	King Essex	King Hunts	King Cambs
Actual ploughs to £s	**0.92**	0.67	0.76	**0.93**	**0.92**	0.51	**0.98**
Potential ploughs to £s	0.89	0.66	0.87	0.92	0.92*	0.57	0.93
Hides to £s	0.81	**0.69**	0.83	0.91	0.78	0.46	0.50
No. entries in sample	63	53	34	17	33	10	21

* Not reliable as potential ploughs frequently not shown.
Notes
   i. The numbers are the writer's count.
   ii. The correlation is made using the Excel 'CORREL' function. The £s relate to the 1086 assessments. The figures in bold show the best correlations.

are used; the correlation is still only 0.91 instead of 0.89. In reality the differences are too small to be statistically significant. In general, the figures show that the ploughlands correlate well with the 1086 assessments; at least they do so in Cambridgeshire. Such correlations are not universally as good (see for instance the figures for Toseland in Table 9). In Cornwall, with much less arable, the correlations of actual ploughlands to £s is about 0.7 and the potential ploughlands to £s about 0.5 (see comments in Appendix E). In Bassetlaw in north Nottinghamshire, with large areas of waste, the equivalent correlations are about 0.5 for actual ploughland and 0.4 for potential ploughlands.

But these samples (in total 231 entries) are too small from which to draw firm national conclusions. The indication, however, is that the Domesday surveyors used the actual rather than potential ploughlands in their main calculations. It may be that potential ploughlands was a lesser factor in those calculations.

We can also note that the correlations of hides to £s are the lowest correlation in each instance for the Domesday entries. This is not surprising as the purpose of the survey was to up-date the assessment of hides and thus the correlation to £s would not be as good. The entire survey would be pointless otherwise. We can see that, for the ICC figures for Armingford, the correlations are not as high comparatively as the Domesday survey figures. The ICC gives every indication in its format that it is a work in progress and this would be consistent with the better correlation for the revised figures in Domesday.

The figures are consistent with the general thesis of this work: that the ploughlands were the primary units of analysis, valuation and assessment. The results are not inconsistent with the Essex analyses of the lay holdings by McDonald and Snook (see their table 1, and comment: 'there is a highly significant relationship between manorial tax assessments and the resources of the manor, with the contribution of the ploughlands being dominant' (1985, 367, 368). Their sample of 695 observations of the lay estates does not include the King's holding in that county while the figures in Table 9 are derived only for the King's land in Essex.[8] Generally, the correlations in Table 9 of actual ploughlands to 1086 assessments above are strong.

4.7 Rental values

Although it seems safe to conclude that the survey is recording or estimating a rack rental value in 1086, it is more difficult to determine exactly how the surveyors arrived at their figures ('rack rent' means the full open market rent or rental value and has no pejorative meaning). As the most important single bit of information in the entry for each manor is the 1086 assessment of value, the question is of some importance. Using as a basis the entries for the manors and a general knowledge of the market in rental values it allows us a limited insight into how the Domesday surveyors arrived at their figures.

The procedures for any valuation require the valuer to make a judgment based on the market evidence. Thus, the procedures in summary are:

i) the collection of market evidence of comparable properties (related to rental evidence in this case) occurring during the relevant period, or applying prior knowledge of the market;
ii) the collection of the value-significant characteristics of those rented properties, or prior knowledge of the productivity factors;
iii) analyses using both sets of data to identify the valuation significant characteristics, assess their relative importance; and
iv) the determination of the level of values for specific types of properties in defined locations using the valuation significant characteristics.

These steps are an essential part of the process of any valuation, including mass appraisals such as Domesday. Perhaps the Domesday surveyors did not

---

8   The use of multiple regression statistical techniques by McDonald and Snook was a welcome innovation. Their figures could have been analysed in a simpler and in a more reader-friendly form. It is not clear what the box/cox transformations add to the average reader's understanding. Nevertheless, the analyses succeed in proving that the Hidage assessments, although rounded, must have related to agricultural productivity and to an ability to pay and were not simply arbitrary figures imposed from above. The figures show the primary importance of the ploughlands and that other factors affected the 1086 value to a lesser extent. However, some of the correlations are inevitable. The area of arable, the ploughland, would certainly correlate with the amount of labour. The land did not farm itself. But, nevertheless, the labour figures recorded in the survey are suspect which makes any analysis of less significance. Appendix B demonstrates the under-recording of farm labour requirements. It is also not clear how the livestock was counted. Appendix C considers the calculation of livestock grazing units. Lastly, the validity of the whole method is thrown into some doubt by the negative correlation of meadow. This does not accord with common sense. Nor is it likely that meadow was exempt from tax. Meadowland was a valuable and necessary asset needed for medieval farming.

have these steps formally in their minds. Nevertheless, this structure would have influenced their thinking, even if the precise process was not formally documented.

4.8 Rental value dispersion

When using rental values as a basis for valuation there is a difficulty. Although the actual rent passing may, in some cases, be the best indication of the rack rent of that property, this is not always so. There are many reasons why properties are held at rents below the market optimum. These reasons can commonly include one or more of the following factors:

- inertia because rents have not been increased over time to reflect changed market values;
- a benevolent attitude by the owner to his tenants;
- a calculated commercial view that rents charged at less than the optimum will result in fewer voids and therefore result in better overall profitability; and of course
- family or personal ties.

Human nature being what it is, we might reasonably guess that all these circumstances would have occurred to some extent in various locations in 1086. This means that, then as now, the widespread of left-skewed evidence for rental values was more difficult to interpret. All values are stochastic. There is statistical noise and there are inconsistencies.

Rents and rental values are, in this respect, different to capital values because it is rare for a vendor selling at arms-length to knowingly sell at a price below the market value. Rents therefore cover a wider range. This point is relevant to Domesday values in three ways. First, it was more difficult for the Domesday surveyors to interpret the scattered rental evidence and settle on an acceptable level for the assessments of rental value. Secondly, it is now more difficult, or maybe impossible, to analyse the levels of assessment and arrive at some algorithm that explains the Domesday surveyors' thought processes. Thirdly it made national consistency of recording and assessment more difficult to achieve.

4.9 The main factors

Three important factors that normally affect agricultural rental values are:

i) soil quality, which determines productivity;
ii) agricultural amenities (such as agricultural buildings which, because they are not listed, we may suppose were excluded in the Domesday assessments); and
iii) access to markets and, particularly, the proximity to urban centres.

County	A central Borough	Total assessments £s	Plough-lands	Value per ploughland (£s)	Straight line distance from London to central borough (km)
Bedfordshire	Bedford	1164	1405	0.83	80
Cambridgeshire	Cambridge	1847	1501	1.23	75
Cornwall	Bodmin	670	1221	0.55	350
Devon	Exeter	3145	5735	0.55	250
Dorset	Dorchester	3110	1858	1.67	180
Hampshire	Winchester	3415	2747	1.24	95
Huntingdonshire	Huntingdon	827	1009	0.82	90
Oxfordshire	Oxford	2878	2584	1.11	85
Somerset	Bath	4361	3924	1.11	160
Wiltshire	Salisbury	4770	3003	1.59	125
Correlation: value of ploughlands to distance from London	−0.46				

TABLE 10. Value and distance from London

In relation to the last of these factors, there is no immediate evidence that the values in Domesday are higher in those vills adjacent to boroughs where demand would have been the greatest. Surprisingly, location within the county may not have been a significant valuation factor or, if it was, Domesday did not take it into account. Compare this with mills where those located in or adjacent to the boroughs of Cambridge and Huntingdon have Domesday values that are markedly higher than average.[9]

However, there is some not very strong evidence that the counties situated further from London (on the assumption that this was the strongest economy) have lower values per plough as shown in Table 10 in ten counties; these were selected because they are not much affected by devastated waste (Fig. 5). There could, of course, be other factors. Perhaps the further west, the greater the rainfall, and then the less conducive it is to arable farming. Perhaps the quality of the soils was a factor. Perhaps rental values were lower because the control over estates was stronger the closer to the seats of power.

---

9 See also the Domesday mills at Battersea (Surrey) with a very high value of £44 9s 8d clearly influenced by the proximity to London. There is little other evidence that can derived from the London area for two reasons. First, London was not included in Domesday. Second, Domesday does not record tide mills which might well have been common on the Thames in tidal locations.

FIGURE 5 Ten county boroughs shown in Table 10

4.10 Soil and land quality

Although we might suppose that the assets used for the assessments are those listed in the survey, there is no indication of the quality of those listed assets. The most significant asset is the soil; the quality of it is central to the assessment of value in Domesday. However, it is difficult to put ourselves in the shoes of the Domesday reeves and farmers. Soil quality, at least for some arable land, is now less important than it once was, even 150 years ago. This is caused by the developments in agriculture. Many physical constraints can now be corrected in part or in whole. Of course, land quality is still significant today and the Grade 1 silts of the Fens are much more valuable than the blow-away sands of the Brecklands, which are situated not very far (about 25 miles/40 km) away. But now productivity for many soils can be greatly improved. Acid soils can be limed, heavy soils effectively under-drained, agricultural operations can be done fast with large modern machines when often short weather windows are favourable and, most importantly, mineral and chemical deficiencies can be corrected with artificial fertiliser.

The Domesday farmers, or indeed the Victorian farmers, had fewer ways of influencing the natural productivity of the soil. For instance, the glacial till chalky Boulder Clay that covers sizeable areas in Huntingdonshire, Cambridgeshire, East Anglia and north Essex is now largely under-drained and provides productive MAFF Grade 2 and 3 arable land that can be readily cultivated with modern farm machinery. These heavy, sometimes intractable, clays would have been much less valuable to the Domesday farmer, especially those lands with little natural gradient and therefore difficult to drain.[10] Probably the undrained silts of the Fens, then providing only summer grazing, were worth less to the Domesday farmer than the well-drained easy workable, but hungry, Brecklands.

In 1086, soil quality, as they then assessed it, must have been a very important factor affecting rental values. It often varies from field to field and, with local knowledge, rental values can reflect this. The Domesday farmers and reeves would certainly have had this knowledge. But it would not be possible to reflect such fine-tuned valuations in a national undertaking on the scale of Domesday. There is always an element of artificiality in *ad valorem* figures assessed in valuation lists for property taxes because of the necessity of achieving comparability for all properties. We can be sure from the general consistency of the methods of assessment in Domesday that there must have been clear central guidance issued about the level of rental values for each circuit and each county.

---

10 An area in West Cambridgeshire known as Hatley Wilds and Croydon Wilds (NGR: TL3052) is an example of chalky Boulder Clay with little gradient. The full arable potential of the soil there was not exploited until mechanical draining with deep ditches and under drains was carried out in the 1940s.

4.11 Assessing agricultural potential

The main valuation considerations that would have determined the agricultural productive capacity of the land of the specified manor in 1086 would probably have been as follows:

- the extent and quality of the arable land;
- the number of plough-teams available to cultivate it;
- the number of labourers available to work the land;
- the amount and quality of meadow land needed to provide hay for the maintenance of the draft animals in winter; and
- the amount of pasture, including woodland grazing, to maintain the stock throughout the year.

These factors are broadly listed in what, in the writer's judgement, might be the order of importance in 1086. In addition, any valuer would want to know the previous tax assessment and details of previous transactions related to the property. The suggested list does, of course, broadly coincide with the order the data are recorded in the survey. However, the valuation relevant information is incomplete.

The analyses in Appendices B and C demonstrate two things. First, the survey does not list the full number of labourers necessary to farm the land or whether they were in fact present. The real agricultural manpower numbers required would be at least five times and perhaps even ten times greater than those specifically listed in Domesday, at least in Cambridgeshire.[11] Secondly, it shows that the survey listing does not directly include the numbers of oxen; the main draft animals. Consequently, the numbers have to be inferred. Then there are listed only the horses used for agricultural purposes and not those used for the transport of people and goods. The grazing requirements for these two groups would have been substantial. The calculation in Appendix C indicates that the land in the areas studied was used quite intensively. On the other hand, a preliminary study of Cornwall in Appendix E suggests that livestock numbers may have been considerably under-estimated in that county and probably this is so generally in the Exeter Book.

The real order of importance of the valuation-significant factors would be determined by empirical evidence (whether through some formal process or through general anecdotal experience). It is clear in Domesday that the extent of the ploughlands was the factor captured in most detail and is recorded in almost every vill entry. Clearly it is the primary valuation-related factor (see Table 9 which demonstrates correlations). The ploughlands were the means of comparison. The other assets listed are all value significant, but to a lesser extent.

---

[11] The factor of five (at least) relates only to the agricultural workforce and not the entire population.

Box 6. Land measurement in the 11th century

We might suppose that some capability to survey and measure land existed in 11th century England. There is, for instance, the entry in *Liber Eliensis* (Fairweather 2005, 11A) which records a dispute about the extent of land in Chippenham, Cambridgeshire, said to be of three hides (perhaps about 360 acres). This was later measured to 226 acres and, within that total, 82 acres were identified as having a problem of title. How would they arrive at these apparently accurate figures without a measured land survey of some sort? In Domesday, there are areas measured to less than a virgate, even sometimes down to an acre, which implies some measurement expertise. See also comments on the variable size of a perch in Lamond and Cunningham (1890, 69).

The Romans had sophisticated land measurement skills and it is unlikely that these were completely lost after the withdrawal of Roman rule, although they were probably less easily available. It has also been noted that the Romans used their land surveying skills for boundary issues only when necessity drove them to do so (Choquer and Favory, 2001, 266). If a landscape was settled and long established, as was the case for Anglo-Saxon England, and the boundaries known by the occupants, there is little point in a general survey. There are also some disadvantages, such as that of igniting dormant boundary disputes. A practice similar to the English 'general boundaries rule' would suffice (Common Law and now s.60 of the *Land Registration Act* 2002).

If, on the other hand, it was an area to be newly settled, then a general survey is necessary to allot the land. Such was the case under Roman rule for lands allotted to veterans and also in America and Australia in the 19th and early 20th centuries for settling lands. However, although the land survey skills then existed, it is likely that they were not widespread in medieval times. Measured land surveys are time-consuming and expensive. They may be necessary where a dispute arises although that alone might not resolve the dispute. They may be desirable for fiscal purposes but they add to the resources required and, consequently, the costs. History has plenty of examples of property taxation systems devised to avoid the necessity of an expensive full land or building surveys. These include 'Peter's pence' on hearths, the later hearth taxes, window taxes and the many levies of aides and subsidies in medieval times based on movables and chattels. We might suppose that the system of taxation based on the concept of the hide used the surveying expertise available to assess the land but did not normally require full land measurement.

It might be hoped that an analysis of all these factors would reveal some mathematical formulae that guided the surveyors, whether specifically laid down in their instructions or as embedded in their professional experience. There have been many commentators who have analysed Domesday but have been no more successful than this work in discovering any underlying numerical basis.

4.12 Exceptions and anomalies

There are three issues which make the analysis of the values recorded in Domesday difficult to interpret. These are:

i) the comparatively high levels of assessment for the holdings of the Royal lands compared with the others;
ii) the higher level of the assessments at TRE compared with 1086 values for many vills, at least in some parts of Domesday; and
iii) that we have no indication of quality of the recorded assets.

4.13 King's direct holdings

There is a marked disparity in the level of the assessments of the King's direct holdings compared with the assessments of other chief tenants, at least in those counties without much recorded waste. It is shown in Table 11. This difference is of significance to the interpretation of Domesday.

In all three counties, the King's holdings are assessed significantly higher per plough than the county mean or the comparable Hundreds and half Hundred (all these mean figures includes the King's holdings). The King's holdings tend to be 1.5 times the mean value of other properties. The differences are certainly more than can have happened by chance. Why might this be so?

TABLE 11. Comparing the Royal holdings

	Mean value per plough
Armingford Hundred in Domesday	£1 5s 0d
Cambridgeshire including Armingford	£1 10s 0d
King's holding in Cambridgeshire	£1 15s 2d
Toseland Hundred	£1 1s 0d
Huntingdonshire including Toseland	£0 15s 3d
King's holdings in Huntingdonshire	£1 11s 0d
Clavering half Hundred	£1 3s 4d
Essex including Clavering	£0 19s 0d
King's holdings in Essex	£1 16s 0d

The first obvious guess is that King William I and his precursors might have acquired and kept the best quality land. As we do not know the boundaries of the King's manors within the vills in which they are recorded in Domesday, it is difficult (but perhaps not impossible) to test this thesis systematically and objectively. Is it possible, however, to make a more subjective judgment? Having looked at the geographic disposition of the Royal holdings in Huntingdonshire, Cambridgeshire and north Essex, the writer's personal opinion, based on his expertise as an agricultural valuer and with a knowledge of the area, is that there is no indication that the value differences result from the king's holdings being located on markedly better quality land than the average holding and certainly not to the degree of difference shown in Table 11.

There are other conceivable explanations. It might be that the surveyors were not assessing exactly the same thing. Perhaps the figures for the Royal holdings included improvements and fixtures such as agricultural buildings and maybe even the other income, such as soke and sake or the Royal equivalent, arising from the ownership of the manor. If so, they were assessing a different legal interest. However, there is no apparent evidence in Domesday to indicate whether or not this was so.

Another possibility is that the king's lands were assessed more forcefully and there is some evidence for this.

> The king let his land at as high a rate as he possibly could; then came some other person, and bade more than the former one gave, and the king let it to men that bid more. Then came a third, and bade yet more; and the king let it to hand to the men that bade him most of all. (*Anglo-Saxon Chronicle* for the year 1087; Ingram and Giles 1847)

The assessments for the royal lands were perhaps what the King expected to receive in annual rents and not a reasonable rental value that might be used as a basis for quota taxes when required. The bases of the assessments of the Royal lands and the underlying philosophy would then be different. The revenues from the Royal estates were considerable in size and of great political importance to the Crown. There would have been every incentive to maximise the return (and that would be difficult in those counties devastated in the 'harrying of the north' (Bates 2016, 313)).

It would suggest therefore that:

i) the King's lands values were based on a different – and wider – legal basis than that for other holdings, and
ii) for the Royal demesne, the survey was in part an aid to estate management.

4.14 TRE assessments

The first fundamental question is what do the TRE numbers represent? Were they the Domesday surveyors' estimates of what the manors would have been worth in rent in 1066? Where they a memory or record of the actual rents

TABLE 12. Comparing Cambridgeshire TRE with 1086 values

	Manors with values decreasing between TRE and 1086	Values remaining the same at TRE and 1086	Manors with values greater in 1086 than TRE
Number	217	157	35
% of such vills in the county	53%	38%	<9%

passing? Were they tax assessments for a tax about which we no longer have any knowledge? The Hidage assessments are not calibrated in money terms and would be of no direct assistance; 20 year old unsupported memories of tax and values are not reliable. In any case, why were the TRE figures required? There are no immediate answers; at least none in Domesday and none that is directly fiscal. There are then difficulties in the interpretation of the TRE values as shown in the example in Table 12.

Thus, surprisingly, the great majority of the values in 1086 in Cambridgeshire are assessed as being lower than the TRE values. The amounts by which they vary show no immediately obvious consistency but the results are significant. For instance, in Armingford Hundred the 1066 TRE values total £238 and the 1086 figures total £204. Cambridgeshire is not unusual. Similar but not identical patterns are found in Huntingdonshire, Bedfordshire, Hertfordshire and in Cornwall, all of which have more manors with values greater at TRE than in 1086. There is no mention of 'waste' in Cambridgeshire and only three references to it in Huntingdonshire (Morris 1975, 27.1, also 19.2 and 19.26) and no indication of any devastation of the landscape in that county after the Conquest.[12] Thus, this does not seem to be the explanation. This is in clear contrast to Yorkshire, and north Nottinghamshire after the 'harrying of the North', or Herefordshire which suffered because of its frontier position next to Wales. TRE values are higher there and this might be expected.[13] So this does not explain the decrease in value in the Eastern counties.

This pattern is hard to explain, but interpretation is made more puzzling when the entries in the Little Domesday Book are considered. In the Clavering half Hundred there are 11 manors with seven of them having values in 1086 greater than TRE; with total values of £38 TRE compared with £49 in 1086: that

---

12   When considering the term 'waste' it is important to distinguish three types of land so described. There is devastated waste caused by destructive actions of humans or through natural disasters. The damage may not be permanent. There is land that is waste because it physically cannot be used beneficially because of its natural character (for instance, it might be too steep or prone to flood). There is also land that is classed as waste only because it was actually unused when the record was made. The three recorded wastelands in Huntingdonshire might fall into one of the last two categories.

13   We can calculate, for instance, that the total TRE values for the Bassetlaw Wapentake in Nottinghamshire were £186, and the 1086 values were £130 (writer's count).

is 30% greater. This is generally typical of Little Domesday which is, therefore, different in this respect from most of the counties in Great Domesday.

Why is there this difference? Was there a fall in values during this 20 year period? If so, why did it not affect the three Little Domesday counties? Was the specification of the assets being valued TRE in the two parts of Domesday identical? Was there a deflation in the value of the currency? Were values unusually low in 1086 due to bad weather? We might first guess that this last factor is so because the *Anglo-Saxon Chronicle* for the year 1086 states that it was 'a swinkful and sorrowful year' (Ingram and Giles 1847). However, such factors would have affected the counties of Little Domesday and the adjoining counties, such as Cambridgeshire, in the same way. If the weather in 1086 was bad for Cambridgeshire, Huntingdonshire and Bedfordshire, it would have been just as bad for Essex and East Anglia. We might suppose that Great Domesday and Little Domesday relate to the same year although there is no certain evidence for this. There are no obvious answers in the Domesday text alone that explains this discrepancy. The best, or perhaps only, explanation is that the surveyors for Little Domesday were using different assessment criteria for the TRE values in those counties. In other words, they were not valuing the same legal interests.

4.15 Assessments when acquired

It is more difficult, or maybe impossible, to make any analysis of the values recorded for 'when acquired' (in abbreviated Latin *qdo recip*) for three reasons. First, there are many manors without any such values recorded. Indeed, there are none in some counties, such as Nottinghamshire. Second, we do not know the date at which the manor was acquired. Third, we do not know from reading Domesday what caused the acquisition and what was the basis of valuation at such events.

Furthermore, why should rental values be of significance on a change of tenure (capital values could well be relevant but not if it was a royal grant for services rendered)? We know that in the normal course of events farms in private occupation tend to change hands within a generation – say about 20 years.[14] The frequency with which the properties changed hands would be similar to the length of the reigns of kings which averages about 20 years in the 250 years after and including Offa. However, the events were not normal immediately after the Conquest. We might therefore suppose that 90% of the manors were acquired within the 20 year period, 1066–1086, and it is statistically certain that some would have changed hands a second time since being first granted by King William. It is not clear whether these monetary figures are actual or estimates, or indeed why they were thought relevant at all.

---

14 The ownerships of the church properties would, of course, have been more stable because institutions are not mortal.

4.16 Quality of the assets

As previously mentioned, Domesday records the existence, the numbers and extent of many classes of assets but it does not overtly record the quality of those assets. However, quality is a factor in any valuation and must have had an influence. To some extent, the classification of uses of land is a proxy for quality, or at least for its productivity. In Domesday, these classifications are in summary: arable land, meadow, pasture and woodland.

The Romans also utilised use-classifications as a proxy for quality for fiscal purposes. In Roman Egypt land for tax purposes was classified as i) irrigated, ii) not irrigated but productive, and iii) not productive; although the tax system was much more complex than this simple classification. Tax was also assessed on output although it is not clear how this was calculated. Was it actual output or an estimated average output (Duncan-Jones 1994, appx 3)? In Roman Gaul, the fiscal categories were arable land of the 1st category, arable land of the 2nd category, meadows, oak forest, ordinary forests and pasture. This is the writer's translation from French (Choquer and Favory 2001, 267). In some respects, this is more sophisticated than Domesday, with two categories of arable land and two of forest.

The Domesday use-classification does not fully allow for quality. Some meadows are more productive than others. Some woodland was more useful than other woodland. In particular, for a list based on agrarian factors, good soils are worth more than poor soils. This might well have been the single most important missing factor in the data collected in Domesday. No doubt the quality of all the listed assets did influence the judgement of the Domesday surveyors, those giving evidence and those who made the final assessment of the values. It may be that the calculation of the extent of a hide or ploughland took the soil quality into account. Perhaps the area of the hide on light hungry lands, like those of the East Anglian Brecklands or the Bagshot Beds in Surrey, was larger than that the size on more productive soils (perhaps like those derived from the Lower Chalk).[15] Nevertheless, it is this important missing dimension that makes it difficult, and perhaps impossible, to discover any exact mathematical formulae using regression or other analyses.

---

15 It is tempting to think that further statistical research might reveal whether this is so. The problems in setting a framework for such research is that we do not know the boundaries of the manors within the vills. Vills, parishes and manors can contain a variety of types and qualities of soils, and it appears that this was often the intention: so that the good lands and the poorer lands were shared. Also, our present-day classification of soils, the MAFF categories, may not accord with the opinions of the 1086 farmers and reeves. Nevertheless, further research might reveal interesting results.

4.17 Unresolved problems: summary

- The King's direct holdings are assessed significantly higher than others. It might be that they are assessed on a different basis.
- The TRE values are higher than 1086 values in Great Domesday but lower in Little Domesday. Perhaps the bases of assessment were different.
- The values 'when acquired' show no pattern and are difficult to explain.
- The quality of the assets recorded are not directly indicated.

4.18 Determining rental levels in Domesday

It seems inconceivable that proposals for such a survey had not been discussed and preparations made before December 1085. The detailed plan for such a large and important enterprise cannot arise fully formed from just one meeting. King William was levying taxes in the period 1066–1086, occasionally if not annually (Harvey 2014 among others). The monks of Ely certainly remembered such taxes.

> Moreover, on his arrival, he imposed an unbearable tax upon the English and, in the same year, gave instruction that a full account of the whole of be written down: how much land each of his barons possessed, how many knights holding lands in fee, how many carts, how many villagers, how many animals – no, how much livestock – each possessed in the whole of his kingdom, from the greatest to the smallest, and how much revenue each property could render. And the land was subjected to harassment, with many calamities following as a consequence. (Fairweather 2005, 209)

It might be supposed these were generally based on the Hidage assessments, and the King was aware of the need for a revaluation. It is not clear to which this year refers. *Liber Eliensis* (the extant version that we have is a copy), was apparently written many years after 1086 and the account may not be accurate on every point. Book 2 of *Liber Eliensis* includes mention of Hereward, who died in about 1072. Was there really a tax that included carts that is now unknown to us? It is more than likely that most taxes (but not all) were based on the Hidage assessments. In which case there would have been a good understanding of the benefits of revising the bases of the Hidage assessments which were, by then, out of date. It appears that there was no national consistency and this was needed. Probably by then, more than about a century since inception, there was more arable land. Many reductions and exemptions had been granted over time. Once granted, it is difficult to remove them except through a complete revaluation. In the writer's opinion, that was an intended purpose of the Domesday survey. Such an important issue must have been considered during the 20 years between 1066 and 1086. In the writer's opinion, there must have been well-advanced draft plans prepared before the 1085 meeting.

As part of these draft plans, the level of values must have been in the mind of those involved in advising the King. Perhaps preliminary enquiries were made about rent levels. More likely, all those involved were well aware of the general rental values because agriculture was the major source of revenue. Just as people now know (or think they know) the value of their house, so in 1086 all those professionally engaged, or with an interest, in the revenue from agricultural land would be aware of rental levels.

The management of the extensive estates from which much of this revenue arose required organisational structures and a flow of information on agriculture, particularly about the success or otherwise of harvests (see Appendix A). Within the land-holding classes, and those who served them professionally, there would have been well-informed (although not necessarily consistent) opinions about agricultural rental levels whether in Cambridgeshire, Cornwall, Huntingdonshire or Herefordshire. Centrally controlled coordination among those in charge of the circuits would have been essential for national consistency. Although there are circuit and county differences in the survey, the general outcome indicates that coordination must have happened from the top and have gone right down the chain of command with great affect. It seems certain that central guidance was given. In summary, it is suggested that the assessed rental values in Domesday for 1086, other than the King's lands, were determined at a reasonable average level, affordable for the average farmer.

4.19 No clear valuation method

In most respects, the attempted analysis of the rental levels is the least satisfactory of all the major issues addressed here. At least, so it seems to a valuer because it never reveals the clarity of method that the Domesday surveyors would have used. The root of this problem is that we do not know exactly what attributes defined a hide and what defined the ploughland as a fiscal unit. This work does not add much to this question apart from identifying the ploughland as being the central fiscal unit of comparison.

For other issues, through analysis of Domesday and supporting texts, we can offer logically derived theses for why Domesday was undertaken, who were the intended taxpayers, what was the taxable property, what was the fiscal unit of comparison, what the 1086 value represented, how long the field survey took to complete and how long the editing and compiling of the Great Domesday and Little Domesday took to complete. It is not clear how exactly the Domesday surveyors progressed from the carefully recorded assets in each manor to an assessed value for that manor in 1086. The general path is clear: from hides to plough-teams to assessed values. The exact mathematical progression is not.

The McDonald and Snook analyses (1985) – multiple regression analyses with box/cox transformations – do indeed prove that the Hidage assessments bear a relation to values and value significant assets. But even without this statistical corroboration it is certain that the Hidage/geld system broadly related to an ability to pay. The tax/geld would not have lasted 170 years and collected large sums of money if that were not the case. That is a fiscal certainty. It would have been otherwise politically impossible to sustain. McDonald and Snook show that the ploughlands were the most important valuation factor, which fits the general conclusions of this publication. Their analyses do not result in an equation or algorithm that allow us to understand what were in the Domesday surveyors' instructions and what was in their minds during the valuation process. Nor is it clear how future research work might change our comprehension.

4.20 Summarised basis of how the manors were assessed

The bases of assessment outside the boroughs were as follows:

- The assessed figures relate to the agrarian value of the manor.
- The assessed values were, or were intended to be, acceptable annual rental values and not the rents passing.
- For valuation purposes, the chosen means of comparison and unit of valuation was expressed as the ploughland.
- All other entries, such as meadow and grazing land, are those that influence and support the opinion of the value of the arable land.
- There were many other valuable non-agricultural assets, which are not recorded and not assessed.
- The value of the growing crops was not included.
- The value of the livestock was not included in the assessment, although the numbers recorded would help the surveyors understand the livestock carrying capacity and determine productive value of the land.
- The full value of the woodland was not included. The only woodland value attributes taken into account are those supporting, directly or indirectly, the agricultural production, particularly that on the arable land. The standing timber values were not captured.
- All the other items, such as the people, the pasture and the meadow which are listed in Domesday, constitute supporting evidence for the single most important entries: the monetary assessments.
- The final 1086 monetary assessments are intended to represent a fair sustainable rental value nationally comparable for all manors.

CHAPTER 5

The Boroughs

5.1 Difficulties of analysis

The boroughs were assessed and recorded in entirely different ways to the rural vills. It is difficult to analyse and compare the boroughs in a methodical way for several reasons. First, there were different customs in the different boroughs. It would be surprising if this were not so. Second, there are many differences in the way assets are listed and the terminology used. Third, the borough descriptions refer to several taxes and sources of revenue, sometimes directly and sometimes by implication. Fourth, although the descriptions of the boroughs have an approximate pattern, the differences are such that it is hard to make schedules of the assets from which comparative statistical analyses can be made of the boroughs. Fifth, the detail of what was recorded varies; see, for instance, the very detailed entry on Colchester and compare this with the sparse detail for Bedford. These observations are well documented by many commentators on Domesday such as Darby (1977, 289 *et seq.*).

There are, however, sufficient common factors to indicate that there were terms of reference and instructions from which the Domesday surveyors worked, and which are now lost to us. It is, in any case, not conceivable that that they were sent out 'blind' without guidance to survey the boroughs. They certainly succeeded in capturing a wealth of raw financial information. Some numbers are shown in Table 13 for some eastern counties boroughs (Fig. 6), listed from south to north, which illustrate the difficulties of making comparative analyses of the borough records using only four sets of statistics.

Taking Table 13 column by column, these show some of the problems that make comparisons difficult. Most boroughs record the number of dwellings and clearly this an important statistic. Therefore, the numbers in column B could be informative and indicate the size of the economy and the population of that borough, if the listings were known to be consistent.[1] Even using only

---

[1] The listings of the dwellings has some relevance to the size of populations. The ratio (population to dwellings) varies depending on economic development. In the UK at present the ratio is about 2.5 persons per dwelling. In 1910 it was about 5. In developing countries it can vary from 7 to more than 10 (this depends on the definition of a separate dwelling). If the factor of persons to dwellings in 1086 was, say, 8–10, it indicates a population for Cambridge of more than 3,000 persons. Compare the Domesday listing of rural persons in Appendix B in Cambridgeshire of 4868. It seems unlikely that about 40% of the county population were living in that borough.

Borough	Taxable dwellings no.	Derelict or not paying tax	Farmland in acres at 120 per hide or carucate	Total value	Value per dwelling
A	B	C	D	E	F
Colchester	538	None listed	3180	£82	37d
Cambridge	373	50	None stated	£15 3s 6d	10d
Huntingdon	261	133	290	£30	28d
Stamford	238	8	1159	£30	30d
Lincoln	924	240	3,031	£100	26d
Torksey	102	111	340	£30	71d
York	1418	None listed	10,080	£100	17d

TABLE 13 Selected figures from seven Boroughs

Note: It is possible to make different interpretations and these figures do not always accord with those from Darby (1977, appx 16) or some other counts.

this small sample, there are reasons why we cannot be certain that this is always so. Dwellings are referred to under four terms (*mansurae, mansiones, hagae* and *domus*). They might or might not be synonymous (Derby 1977, 294). The Lincoln listing refers to houses being counted in the 'English way', which appears to mean that 120 houses counted for tax purposes as 100. This method is not mentioned in the other boroughs but we cannot be sure that only Lincoln used it. For Lincoln, the figure shown is the gross number, not the net for tax total. In Torksey, the number of houses is not directly stated and is deduced from the number of burgesses. There are indications in the Torksey text that the burgesses had houses. Perhaps other boroughs had houses occupied by burgesses in addition to the number of dwellings listed.

The number of derelict buildings in column C is certainly informative, especially for Lincoln where some were unoccupied or derelict for economic reasons. However, no derelict buildings are listed in Colchester or York. It is not clear from Domesday alone whether this is a difference in the method of listing or whether there really were no derelict buildings there. That would be unlikely.

For agricultural land in column D, in Cambridge no farmland is listed although it is likely it existed within the city limits and ploughs are mentioned. On the other hand, some of the farmland in Stamford was outside the city boundaries. Colchester is unusual because it lists more than 120 separate land holdings, some no more than 1 acre. There is no clear indication of whether the farmland influenced the final totals and, if so, by how much.

The apparent borough totals, such as they are, are shown in column E. In both Colchester and York there are listed other amounts, sometimes from outside the borough, which might be added but are not in Table 13. It seems unlikely that Cambridge was worth less than Huntingdon or Torksey. In any case, Torksey seems to be a statistical outlier.

The values from column E are divided by the number of dwellings in column B. The result is the value per listed dwelling in money, d (pence) in column F.

5. The Boroughs 81

FIGURE 6 Location of seven boroughs

It seems to show some semblance of a pattern; of 26d to 37d per dwelling. But Torksey, Cambridge and York are outside this range. However, for the entire range, the correlation of the number of dwellings in each borough to the value is still 0.86. Although Table 13 relates to only 3850 dwellings, we can say that the number of dwellings was clearly the main determinant of the quantum of tax revenue, but it was not the sole factor.

Lincoln and Colchester are the only ones in this sample which devote space to rent arrears and so no general comparison can be made. These entries, together with the *Inquisition Gheldi* in *Liber Exoniensis* (Welldon Finn 1964), support the thesis that Domesday is a fiscal document. These entries about arrears are also useful illustrations of the perennial and universal difficulties of collecting tax.

5.2 Summary of borough analyses

It is clear that the urban parts of the boroughs were surveyed and assessed on a different basis to the other, rural, vills. This would have to be the case because these sections are not agrarian lists. Notwithstanding the widely recognised analytical problems, it is possible to list several common factors and common differences. In summary they are these.

1. The monetary values listed are rents paid or rent due, or other sources of annual revenue. They are not the rental values as is the case for the rural manors. This is an important distinction.
2. The boroughs paid an amount every year and not only when a special geld was levied.
3. The body primarily liable for tax is the borough itself, as represented by the burgesses, rather than the individual persons (sometimes identified) living or owning property within the borough and paying the rents or dues.
4. The borough revenues did not all go to the King. Some went to powerful men. The division of parts of the revenues is quite frequently clearly stated. See, for example, Lincoln with the King and Earl Hugh sharing the revenue, perhaps two-thirds to one-third. Some revenues must have remained in the boroughs to defray the cost of administration and other expenses for which they were responsible.
5. For houses (often *mansiones, mans.* Abr) which description no doubt also included commercial, or partly commercial, buildings, the amounts listed are something similar to an annual ground rent tax based on the plot. It is not the rent or rental value of the building.
6. Tax was apparently not generally due if the house was derelict. This makes fiscal sense because there were in such cases no occupiers from whom tax could be extracted. There are however exceptions to this general rule.
7. There are other taxes and sources of revenue listed such as tribute (*landgable*), toll, forfeiture, heriot, the King's tax. There might have been many more sources of tax and revenue. For instance, there is one mention in Torksey

of exemption from dues on similar to *octroi*[2] on goods passing in and out of the boroughs (Morris 1986, T). Perhaps there were other taxes of which we are not aware. Other non-tax sources of revenue, such as market dues and moneyers' fees, are often listed.

8. There are agricultural lands attached to some boroughs and, when listed, they are often quoted in hides apparently in the same manner as the vills. They are not then generally reassessed to actual and potential ploughlands as in the rural manors (although there are exceptions; see, for instance, one in Colchester). Such a step would have been unnecessary as the surveyors were concerned with the actual rents and not an assessed value as a basis for a quota tax as was the case for rural manors.
9. Mills are listed with what is presumably the rental income. In respect of Cambridge, clearly the rental income is not included in the borough total. It is not clear how mills were assessed either in the boroughs or the rural vills, and how and when tax was collected on them.
10. The monetary totals, which we might have supposed were the most important item, are not yet universally consistent.

5.3 Comparison with Burghal Hidages

As noted above, when looking at the borough listings, unlike the rural manors, we do not find that they all have reliable consistent monetary totals. Compare this situation with the comparatively precise assessments of burghal Hidage of 33 Wessex boroughs produced in or before 911 (Maitland 1989, 502). It should be noted that the burghal Hidages in that document were based on a specific stated need (that is, to build and maintain fortification walls in those boroughs), rather than ability to pay, as was the purpose of Domesday. This is a significant difference. Burghal Hidages were about the distribution of the revenue from a geld; rather than a contribution to it.[3] Nevertheless, the hide unit was used. Probably this was all they had.

5.4 Collecting the information

As the boroughs were yielding annual revenues to the King, it might be that much of that information was already held centrally. However, we might suppose that visits to most of the boroughs were made by the commissioners and their appointed deputies. The detail in the Colchester records seems to show this (although they do not seem to have spent much time in Bedford). Furthermore, the information about derelict houses might be evidence of visits. Dereliction

---

2 Octroi is a form of internal customs dues, originally one-eighth of the value. It was common in many countries in the medieval era and on into the 19th century. It is now rare. The writer encountered it in only one location in one country in his career.
3 The majority of the burghal totals are shown in tens or hundreds of pounds, so there was a rounding of the assessments.

is not a permanent state and changes constantly. The boroughs would want to indicate the derelict houses in 1086 to reduce the amount of taxation.

5.5 Use and purpose

We might suppose that the boroughs were surveyed for the same purpose as the remainder of the Domesday survey: and that purpose is fiscal. That is why they are part of the survey. That is why the boroughs are listed in the counties within which they are situated. The borough surveys are clearly concerned with several sources of revenue within the boroughs and, as in the rest of the survey, they only deal with matters of title – when they do so – as a consequence of the fiscal purpose.

However, as noted above, in one important respect it appears they differ from the rest of the survey in that the sources of revenue listed are mostly annual taxes and annual revenues rather than assessments for a quota tax paid when circumstances required revenue beyond the King's normal annual sources.

The broad fiscal purpose of the survey for the boroughs was, it might be supposed, no different from the purpose of the survey for the rest of Domesday. It was to determine the boroughs capacity to pay but, in these cases, annually. If so, was it also to determine how much of the national share of a geld that borough could contribute to a quota tax additionally in time of crisis? How did it fit with a geld? It could be that some of the sources of revenue listed were paid annually to the King and a periodic geld was levied in relation to other sources of tax and revenue. Perhaps this issue had yet to be determined when the survey was being made.

5.6 Incomplete record

First, it seems clear that the normal survey format of Domesday did not suit the boroughs, and secondly that central government had less control over the urban settlements. For these and other reasons it is reasonable to suppose that the returns of the boroughs that have come down to us in Domesday were not meant to be the final versions. The wealth of captured raw financial data could have been ruthlessly edited and reduced to a single consistent monetary assessment for each borough comparable with the rural assessments. This would have been no simple task because of the many variations. Nevertheless, the precision of the burghal Hidages could have been replicated. The entries for London and Winchester and other missing boroughs would then have been added at another stage.[4] We might guess that this was the intended plan. The assessments would then have been usable as part of the entire national tax base. This seems to be the only way to make sense of the borough returns.

---

4   The sources of revenue from London and Winchester would, in comparison with other boroughs, have been greater and more varied but more difficult to list and to assess. Politics in these powerful boroughs might have made access more difficult.

CHAPTER 6

The logistics

6.1 The logistic framework

Property taxes in one form or another have been in existence for at least two millennia and perhaps existed even 5000 years ago in China. There are, today, property taxes of some sort in most countries of the world and there are logistical commonalties. There is much known about the administration of the tax. Implementations occur in a number of well-known and well-tried stages, which are identified in Table 14.

There are important points to take from this table. All the steps listed are general actions that are necessary for the completion of any valuation or property tax list in any age in any country. None of the actions is optional. The steps are set down in Table 14 with the Domesday survey in mind and, in other circumstances, the exact description of the actions might be expressed in slightly different words. But each one of the legal, valuation and logistic steps must be carried out in some manner if the property list is to be completed. We know that many attempts to implement a tax, or carry out a revaluation, fail because just one of the above steps fails; like a broken link in a chain. The Domesday survey did not fail administratively. Therefore, there is no doubt that all the above listed steps up to row 16 were taken in order to complete the survey in the form that we know it.

This is not to say each action must be newly initiated for every property tax valuation or revaluation. The legal authority for the tax may already be available. It was so for Domesday; the Royal command sufficed. All taxable properties and all taxpayers must be identified as in rows 10 and 11 of Table 14. This can be a time-consuming task. In the case of the Domesday survey, the surveyors used (and revised as necessary) the already available information from the Hidage assessment system, which made the task much simpler and facilitated a shorter timetable.

Note also that Table 14 is to some extent incomplete as a fiscal procedure. All property taxes are supported on a tripod of three elements: assessment, collection and enforcement. The failure of any of these elements results in the failure of the whole tax (and this often happens). Although rows 17 and 18 refer to these last two of these elements they are not listed in detail because no tax was ever collected directly from the survey.

The general point to take from Table 14 is that the imposition, execution and maintenance of a land taxation system (or any tax system) requires political will and determination, logistical organisation and professional

	Actions	Comments relevant to Domesday	Other parallel, sometimes independent, actions occurring at the same time
	A	B	C
1	Make the political decision to implement a tax or to carry out a revaluation	This was solely the King's decision	
2	Determine and implement the legal basis of the tax	The final form of the tax seems to have been approved at the meeting in Gloucester at Christmas 1085. The King's command was the legal basis	
3	Decide on the appropriate timetable		Identify the valuation significant characteristics to be captured for each class of property
4	Plan the logistics of the campaign		Assemble valuation evidence: such as the level of agricultural rents passing
5	Set up an organisation to implement the campaign		Analyse valuation evidence
6	Appoint key personnel commissioned with relevant responsibilities	Actions 3–6 might have been achieved at the Christmas 1085 meeting	
7	Recruit and appoint other staff		Decide on assessed values
8	Inform and instruct County officials and others about what is required from them and when		
9	Deploy teams in the field	It is considered that full deployment could not have been achieved before April 1086 if the 1085 Christmas meeting was the starting point	Instruct teams on how they will carry out their tasks
10	Identify all taxable properties	It appears that the great majority of the taxable properties were those already assessed under the hidage system. Therefore, only a limited amount of additional action was required	Issue guidance on levels of value to teams
11	Identify all taxpayers	As above	
12	Capture valuation significant data for every taxable property	The results are as in the ICC and Domesday	
13	Value every taxable property		
14	Make a draft valuation list containing the tax base (i.e. all the valuations)		
15	Edit and re-edit as required		
16	Finish the valuation list		
17	Start tax collection	No evidence that this ever happened	
18	Enforce tax collection	Therefore, not applicable	

TABLE 14 (opposite). Valuation list logistics: a general framework

expertise; and the Domesday survey clearly displays the successful results of these characteristics.

6.2 Logistical issues

There are related material matters that must be addressed when organising any first valuation or revaluation. It is possible to identify the main logistical issues. We do not know how they were resolved but we know that they all were because we have the Domesday Books as evidence. This result could not have been achieved without the logistics being in place. An outline of those basic issues that had to be addressed by the commissioners for Domesday are set out below.

Pre-conditions

i) The timetable, or often in practice the date by which the task is to be completed, must be established. We do not know when the Domesday task was commenced. We can be sure it was not fully finished in 1086. We cannot be sure of the intended timetable but the timetable affects all the other logistical issues. Therefore, we now cannot precisely model the logistics of the supply because we do not know the exact timetable. The logistic model below is intended to find out if it could have been done within the calendar year of 1086.

ii) The size of the task must be estimated, in particular the number of taxable properties. The commissioners would have known the size of the Hidage assessment system. We know the size of the Domesday Books now extant. We do not know the additional material that was collected but that was either not used or discarded in the final draft. If we compare the material in the ICC with that in Domesday or the material in Little Domesday with that in Great Domesday, we might suppose that more information was collected than appeared in the final drafts available to us. The commissioners would have a good idea of the size of the task.

Issues of supply

These are outlined in Table 15.

Deployment

For each of the specific matters above decisions must be made about the quantities required, and exactly when and where they are to be deployed and who was responsible for making this happen.

The above remarks and the issues listed in Table 15 are approximate indications only of the logistics and included to illustrate the size and scope of the organisational issues that had to addressed to complete the survey. Clearly the issues were successfully addressed as the existence of the Domesday Books shows.

General issue	Specific issue	Comments relevant to DB
Personnel	Numbers required to complete the work within the timetable	See calculations in tables below
	Professional skills	This is a difficult issue. We know the scale and character of the survey. We can be sure that this outcome required a large team of surveyors and the application by them of various skills and the possession of technical knowledge, including that of agriculture, agricultural values and land tenure. We may wonder whether all those skills were already available on the scale required prior to the surveys. If not, there would have been a considerable amount of training and tuition required which would have required time and organisation. We might therefore guess that the skills were generally already available for the administration of the hidage and geld system
	Training and instructions	In any event, even if the skills were already present, there would have been the need for careful briefings to ensure compliance with the detailed capture of the data for this particular task
	Language skills	Although the *lingua franca* was Latin, we might suppose that other language skills must have been required. Not all would have Latin. The written and oral knowledge of the hidage system would, we might guess, have been in English. Enquiries made at a local level and evidence taken would have been in several languages: pre-Conquest English, French and perhaps Danish in the former Danelaw areas
Transportation		There are the journeys from, and back to, the home bases for the surveyors and their supporting teams. There would have also travelled within the counties in which they were working. There might have been travel to Winchester on more than one occasion.
Writing materials	Parchment	Calculations have been made of the material required for the drafts of the surveys that are extant. For Great Domesday there are 200 leaves requiring almost as many sheep. At least three times as much would be required for the initial capture of the data and the subsequent editing notes. Production of parchment is not a quick process. We do not know if such supplies, which might amount to 800 leaves, were normally held in stock in the necessary quantities or had to be specially manufactured or were to be procured elsewhere
	Quills	As above although more easily procured
	Ink	As above although more easily procured
Material issues	Subsistence and accommodation for the investigating teams	We might suppose that this was supplied by the Shire Reeves when the teams were within their county
Other material issues	Security	We might suppose that this was supplied by the Shire Reeves

6.3 Physical inspections

It seems that most commentators on Domesday suppose that all the information for the survey was gathered in legal hearings before a local jury with evidence given under oath. Most of the commentators on the survey generally seem to be under the unstated impression that judicial hearings could collect the data and make judgements faster at court hearings than by physical on-site inspections. Those with

TABLE 15 (opposite).
Logistics and supplies

first-hand experience of land-based litigation and the often time-consuming court procedures, when compared with physical inspections and surveys of land and real property might, like the writer, think this opinion seriously misplaced. However, the naming of the persons who swore – the so-called jurors (in some parts of Domesday and ICC) – seems to be the grounds for supposing that there were hearings of some sort somewhere. This supposed simplistic scenario (of nothing but jury hearings) needs analysis. The first element of analysis is the classification of the several elements of the survey. There were known existing data to be captured or recaptured such as the identification of the manors (the taxable unit) and the Hidage assessment applicable to them. There was the legal or *de facto* matter of identifying the taxpayer. There were physical matters to be determined such as the number of ploughlands and the size of pastures, meadows or woodlands and the number of livestock. There were physical matters on which a judgement has to be made: in particular, the numbers of ploughlands there could be on that manor as compared with the actual number. There was then the most important matter of judgement to be made: the rental value in 1086. The magnitude of these tasks, which are relevant to each of 21,000 manors, is considerable.

Then the second dimension of the analysis is that there are the three parties involved:

i)   the tenants-in-chief (the taxpayers),
ii) the assessors,
iii) others, including the persons who are listed as those who swore; perhaps they can be termed jurors, although this is misleading.

We can be sure that, in most cases, it was not usually the tenants-in-chief personally and locally giving evidence. Most of the land was held by the large landowners (see Appendix D for examples). It would have been physically impossible for the large landowners personally to provide evidence of all their manors to the assessors. The task of representing them would have mostly devolved to their seneschals, reeves, bailiffs or other men. Perhaps there were some written returns as others have suggested, but this is unlikely to be have been entirely reliable, universal or even a widespread practice.

The assessors, that is those commissioned to carry out the survey or their many appointed deputies, must have been those who made judgements about the physical facts and of values. The number of possible ploughlands requires judgement: it is not a fixed and certain size. Values are stochastic. They are not some fixed easily identified quantity known to all.

It seems very unlikely that all the Domesday questions were determined by juries or even that juries as we know them were constituted for the survey. Juries were used in the 12th century in relation to land disputes and possibly before that. Unlike a modern jury, their role is thought to have been investigative and not adjudicative. The concept of an impartial jury coming fresh on the scene to give a verdict only in accordance with the evidence given before them is much more modern (Pollock and Maitland 1959, vol. 1, 138).

For Domesday perhaps the best indication comes from the ICC. It lists for each Hundred certain named men, usually nine in number, who gave oath or who swore.[1] Also, in Huntingdonshire it states at the beginning of the 29 declarations – '*Dicunt homines qui jurauer*', which could be translated as 'So said the men who gave evidence under oath'. (This is the writer's translation which does not accord with Morris 1975, D). In the ICC generally the wording is *iurauerunt homines* followed by the names. Many individuals in the ICC are identifiable as local men and maybe they all had some connection to that Hundred. We might guess that is why they were called. Some of them are stated to be the men of the landowners. After those specifically named men giving evidence it adds, in Otway-Ruthven's translation in the Cambridgeshire VCH volume 1, the phrase *and all French and Englishmen* (Sulzman 1938, vol. 1, 400: 427; Otway-Ruthven 1938): and also for Thriplow in the introduction in Phillimore: *et onis alii fraci et angli* , 'and all other Frenchmen and Englishmen' (Morris 1981, D).

We might suppose only the most important persons giving evidence were named. These bodies of men of indeterminate number do not look to be adjudicative juries. The recorded names are, however, quite in keeping with a listing of those who gave evidence under oath; or least the important men who gave evidence. Truth and accuracy were made more likely by a) taking evidence under oath and b) naming those on record of doing so.

There is also abundant evidence in Domesday that those giving evidence (possibly the jurors but only in a wide sense of the term) had an input as to their opinion on matters of title. These are their opinions and not determinations of fact. However, it is hard to find any evidence in Domesday of them commenting on or determining matters related to physical facts. Perhaps the identification of title or naming the legitimate occupier was their main role. Perhaps this was their only role. Similarly, it is difficult to find any evidence that they routinely determined or questioned the accuracy of the data being gathered or that they made judgements on matters of value. That really could not have been their role. National consistency of approach would not have been possible if it was. Absence of evidence is, of course, no proof that they had only such a limited role mainly related to matters of title but, on the other hand, this absence does not support the general view, indeed almost universal view, that the data was gathered at judicial hearings only.

The thesis put forward here is that the vills must have been inspected at some point, because, how else could such a body of data be captured and recorded with such consistency; and in such detail? There are five grounds on which this supposition is supported.

Self-assessment not feasible

If the survey relied solely on judicial hearings, it is not clear how they might have been conducted. One theoretical option is that the sole source of the

---

[1] Although in the ICC there are mostly nine named persons who swore, there are four vills in which eight names are given and one vill with only seven.

evidence (verbal or written) about the many facts recorded, including values, was given by tenants-in-chief and other landholders or their representatives at these hearings. This would be similar in character to self-assessment for taxation. Self-assessment in taxation procedures has its limitations, especially if there is a large amount of opinion-based information being sought and this was the case for Domesday. Even if every landholder (or their representatives) were honest, not every landholder would interpret the large number of questions in the same way. They might reasonably construe them in the manner most favourable to themselves. Absentee landlords would not necessarily know all the details. It cannot be assumed that all were honest. Of course, the local knowledge of the men giving evidence could moderate the findings but there would have been limits to that body of knowledge. Furthermore, there would have been little control of local collusion. It is not easy to see how all the information captured in, for instance the ICC, could have been done only at court hearings. There are no examples of this much data being universally captured for 22,000 taxable properties by self-assessment or by judicial hearings without site inspections anywhere else at any time known to the writer.

Shire Reeve assessment not impartial

A second theoretical course of action is hearings as above, with the Shire Reeve using his power and local knowledge to moderate and interpret the evidence given. Picot, the Shire Reeve for Cambridgeshire, would have known the lands of the county well and appreciated their worth. We can be sure of this because he clearly expended much effort in acquiring large holdings of land for himself. In Cambridgeshire, he held 44 manors as tenant-in-chief (of which 23 were sub-let) worth £139 or 7.5% of the county total. He also held about 20 manors as sub-tenant from others and presumably profited from them. In addition, he built and held a mill in Cambridge.[2] He was not disinterested. He was not universally popular as this extract from *Liber Eliensis* reveals:

> Well then, the county of Cambridge had fallen by chance to the lot of Picot, a Norman by race, a Gaetulian by temperament. A staving lion, a footloose wolf, a deceitful fox, a muddy swine, an impudent dog – in the end he obtained the food which he had long hankered after and, if the whole county was one carcass, he claimed it all for himself, took possession of the of it and, like an insatiable monster bent on transferring the whole of it to his belly, did not allow anyone to be sharer of his portion – not God not an angel, none of the saints, no – and this is what I am leading up to – the most holy and famous AEthelthryth, who up till then had owned a great many properties – lands or vills – in that same county, by gift and grant of prominent people of former times. (Fairweather 2005, book II, 1312)

---

2 Domesday lists Picot as owning three mills. However, this does not mean there were three separate free-standing buildings, although there might have been three millstones. *Liber Eliensis* refers to only one mill for Picot. We might guess that this was at Newnham.

It is unlikely that the monks of Ely were alone in their opinion. Perhaps not all Shire Reeves were as acquisitive or as disliked as was Picot. Nevertheless, no Shire Reeve would necessarily have been an impartial and disinterested party (see Appendix G). It would have been unwise to take the views of every one of them at face value. There is also the need for national consistency throughout Domesday. Shire Reeves would inevitably have their own views on levels of value and other matters. As already observed, values are stochastic and subject to different opinions. These opinions would not necessarily be consistent one with another. It is hard to see how the work of the Shire Reeves could be scrutinised for either accuracy or consistency between counties through local jury hearings only. Neither objective could be achieved, without some field visits involving the Domesday surveyors.

Geographic order

In has been noticed that, in the ICC, the Hundreds are listed in what might be a geographic order of travel. For those Hundreds for which records survive in ICC, the sequence is as follows: *Staploe; Isleham; Cheveley; Staine; Radfield; Flendish; Chilford; Whittlesford; Thriplow; Armingford; Wetherley; Papworth; Northstow.*

Round (1909) argued that the above sequence suggests that the judicial hearings were held in the Hundreds, rather than in Cambridge, and the order reveals the route travelled by the assessors. This argument seems compelling. If so, the assessors were at least close to the lands which they were assessing.

Did they inspect the individual vills? In all the Hundreds (for which records survive) in the ICC, the order in which the vills are listed is a 'walking order'. For example, in Armingford Hundred (Fig. 7) the vills are listed in ICC in the following order: *Steeple Morden; Tadlow; Guilden Morden; Clopton; Hatley; Croydon; Wendy; Shingay; Litlington; Abington Pigotts; Bassingbourn; Whaddon; Meldreth; Melbourn.*[3]

Hart (1974) notes the order of the vills in the ICC, which is also sometimes shadowed in the Domesday, within the tenants-in chief lists.[4] But he does not remark on the geographical significance. The significance is that the listed sequence is in a feasible walking order. It is not perfect. Why go from Steeple Morden to adjacent Guilden Morden via Tadlow? But for reasons that we will never know, it might well have occurred that way. It is not much out

---

3   The order of listing of other vills in the ICC are shown in Hart (1974). It is also found in Phillimore for Cambridgeshire (Morris 1981).

4   A travelling order as seen in the sequence of the manors as listed in the holdings of the King or tenants-in-chief is sometimes apparent and sometimes not so. For instance, in the Bassetlaw wapentake in Nottinghamshire there is a clear geographic order for 62 out of 66 manors of the King's holdings. The last four listings lie outside his main block of royal manors in Bassetlaw.

of the way. There is no other obvious explanation why the vills are listed in this order unless this was the order in which they were actually inspected. The same applies to the vills in all the other Hundreds recorded in the ICC. They are all in a walking order to a greater or lesser extent. It is also significant the last listed vill in most Hundreds in the ICC is commonly geographically close (and sometimes adjacent) to the first listed vill in the next Hundred. This also indicates a travelling order.

Format of ICC

The ICC is arranged first by vills. If it was a record of inspections of every vill in the field this is exactly how the results would be recorded. Each vill entry starts with a statement of the Hidage assessment of the whole vill. This information would have been already established and known but would have been a good starting point for an enquiry in the field. It then lists the required items related to individual manor owners and the apportionment of the Hidage. Its format is entirely consistent with a visit to the vill and an enquiry made there of the inhabitants.

Valuation and other judgements

Some things are not, in practice, ascertainable by juries. At least not unless they have before them expert (or at least well-informed) evidence from those who have made a recent physical inspection of the land. There are in Domesday and the ICC estimates and valuation judgements which are:

i) the estimate of the number of ploughlands that there could be in that manor rather than those that actually are there, and
ii) the value of the land. It is not obvious how such judgements could be made without a visit to the vill or that this important item could be determined by evidence given in court. There would have been no consistency. The Domesday values show a national consistency of approach.

The above five grounds seek to support and rationalise a professional opinion based on practical experience; that the compilation of such a list would not have been possible without physical inspection at some stage. Many of the facts are to be found only in the field. It is a thesis that is further supported by the writer not being aware of any property valuation list of this size and this purpose, anywhere in the world, at any time, being compiled without physical inspection.[5] Why should we suppose that Domesday was an exception?

---

5   Now this inspection can be by satellite imagery.

94   *Surveying the Domesday Book*

1. Steeple Morden
2. Tadlow
3. Guilden Morden
4. Clopton
5. East Hatley
6. Croydon
7. Wendy
8. Shingay
9. Litlington
10. Abington Pigotts
11. Bassingbourn
12. Whaddon
13. Meldreth
14. Melbourn

FIGURE 7 The vills in Armingford Hundred

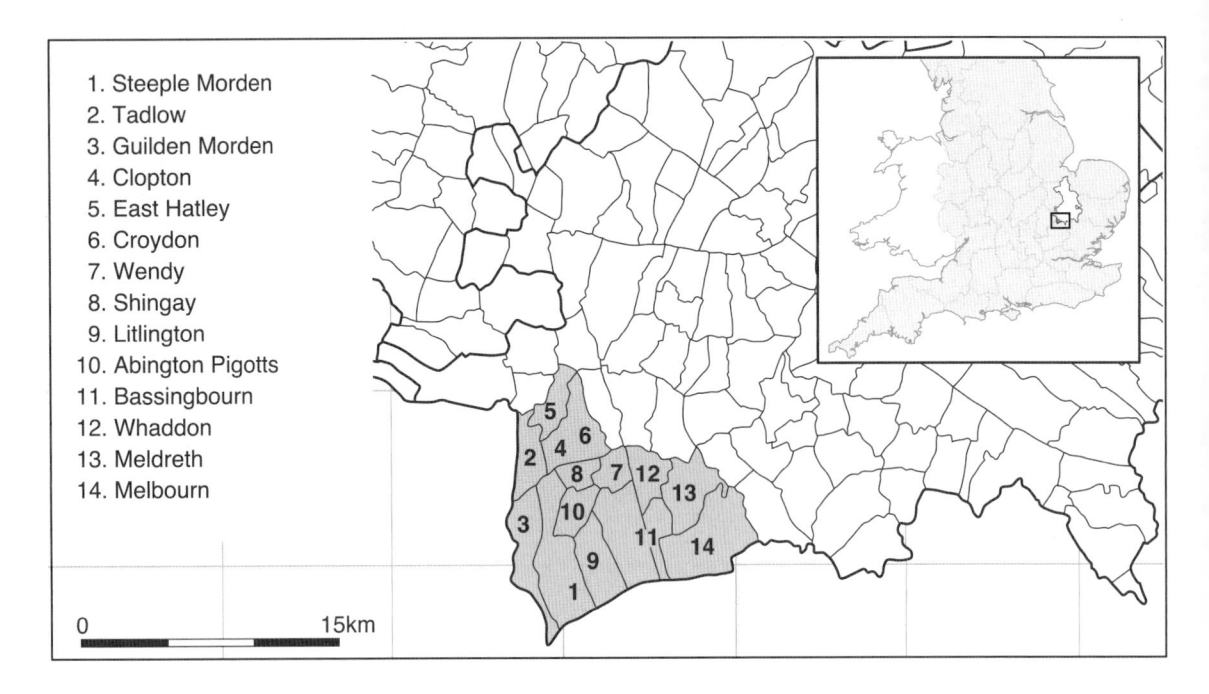

6.4 The sequence of events

The sequence and order of a property list is important. If designed well the users of the list will be able to locate the information and items sought and will give little thought to the design. The Domesday Books have defined categories, a hierarchy and orders within those categories: and they are not alphabetically or numerically ordered. They were designed with exactitude. The hierarchy starts with the counties; a geographical category with the order of listing probably relating to the circuits. The subsequent categories within each county are the tenants-in-chief; a social category listed in order of feudal rank. Within the entry to each tenant-in-chief in that county, his/her manors are listed by Hundreds; a geographical order. There are then the legal, fiscal and geographical categories within each manor. Although the final order of the Domesday entries is largely consistent it does not mean that the data were collected in that specific order. This is clear from the ICC.

There is no direct evidence of the exact sequence of events that took place during the Domesday survey. Table 14 gives a general framework and it is not specific to Domesday and is not a timetable. An examination and comparison of the structures and contents of the ICC, *Liber Exoniensis*, Little Domesday (for Essex in this study) and the Cambridgeshire Domesday gives an indication of how the data could have been captured and edited, and then re-edited and written-up in a fair copy. This interpretation is based on those written formats now available to us and are as follows:

- The first action was the capture of data in the field. The ICC is consistent with the first capture of the data as it might have been written in a field book. The structure of the document is as follows:
  i) County
  ii) Hundred
  iii) Vill
  iv) Landholders
- The second action was the verification of the data and comments under oath on matters of title at a judicial hearing, possibly held in the vill during the visit.
- The third action, presumably at a central point, is the first editing of the data captured in the field and at any judicial hearings. The results are consistent with the format of Little Domesday. There is the fundamental re-ordering of units from the vills to the individual tenants. The reversals of the two last parts of the structure are significant. Structure:
  i) County
  ii) Landholders, in listed in order of rank with his (or her or their) holdings in each Hundred
  iii) Each vill of the land holder separately listed and assessed.
- A further editing would have taken place and the result could accord with the format similar to that of *Liber Exoniensis*.
- The subsequent actions are further editing, possibly in several stages, and the removal of data about livestock. There is no record of the outcomes of these stages.
- The final action is the production of a fair copy, apparently in a single hand, of the edited version of the data, as in Great Domesday.

It would have been possible to further edit what we now regard as the final version. A more easily usable fiscal format would have a list containing only the manor, the tenant/taxpayer and the assessment. Such a list would contain the essential data required for a tax cadastre without the supporting evidence. In other words, it would have looked like a modern property tax list. It would have had several advantages. It would be simpler to use as a valuation list. It would be easier to revise. There is no evidence that this was ever considered (and see also the comments above on the Boroughs which suggest that the version we see there was not intended to be the final one).

6.5 The ICC as a precedent

As has been noted by Round (1909), the ICC is crucial to the understanding of Domesday: and this is the writer's opinion. There is a structure in the listed ICC data. Each vill starts with the overall Hidage for that vill and that is thereafter apportioned to each manor within the vill. The tenants and sub-tenants are each listed sequentially in each vill. There is much information about tenure

TABLE 16. Armingford Hundred comparisons

	No. plough-teams	Values	Value per plough-team
ICC	169	£153	18s 1d
Domesday	182	£204	£1 2s 5d

and roots of title which is not always easy to follow. Livestock is included, although it should be viewed subject to the comments in Appendix C. However, the document is not simple to interpret. Because of the way it is written, the contents are not easily reduced to categories with any certainty. Nevertheless, an analysis (by entering every entry into a spreadsheet) has been carried out and a comparison made between the listings in ICC and Domesday for the Armingford Hundred. There are difficulties because two of the Hundreds are missing and there are other losses. For instance a page in the Longstowe Hundred is missing so we cannot compare, for instance, the Gamlingay parish and vill with the Domesday entry. Nevertheless, much of the data can be matched from ICC to Domesday and there are some significant differences, two of which are shown in Table 16.

Might the increase in the number of plough-teams and values indicate that the ICC survey preceded Domesday? It is unlikely that that the Domesday surveyors and Commissioners would reduce the number of plough-teams and the assessed value per plough-team. It is more likely that those supervising the original surveyors reviewed the first assessments and increased them where they considered it necessary. Nor is it likely that the extra historic information about titles was added after Domesday. There is every indication that ICC pre-dated the Domesday survey of Cambridgeshire. The sequence accords with a general view. However, it is argued that ICC is a record of a physical visit to the vills and not a record of judicial hearings in the Hundreds.

This sequence of events is important for the analysis presented here although we can never know for certain what actually occurred. There are different options and permutations and the ICC gives us some clues.

For the survey there are four possibilities.

i) No new physical surveys were made in the vills. This scenario is rejected for the reasons stated in Section 6.3 above.
ii) It might be that regular surveys and visits were being made continually for the administration of the Hidage assessments and the data already existed. This option is possible but it is unlikely that any visits prior to the Domesday process would have been capturing the detail we now see in ICC, the Exeter Book and both Domesday Books.
iii) It could be that country-wide surveys were carried out prior to Christmas 1085 in anticipation of Domesday and the data captured in the format of ICC. If so, all but Cambridgeshire are now lost to us. This is a logically

feasible option and would suggest a realistic timetable. But it is supported only by the existence of ICC and to a lesser extent by the Exeter Book.
iv) Physical surveys of all the 13,000 vills were carried out in 1086 and the data recorded in manner of the ICC. The logistics of this option are examined below.

For the process of giving evidence there are three possibilities.

a) Evidence might have been given only in a series of hearings in the county town. Although this option is possible there is no evidence to support it.
b) Evidence might have been given at separate hearings in each Hundred. The men who gave evidence are named and listed in ICC. There is a different body of men for each Hundred which are listed in a traveling order. This is a logistically feasible option and it fits with the limited evidence we have.
c) Evidence might have been given only during each visit of the commissioners or their surveyors to the vills using the procedures and facilities of the manor courts. This is by far the simplest and quickest option. It is not contradicted by any of the evidence. It has the complication that the eight men of the Hundred giving evidence would have had to travel to each vill with the commissioner or surveyors. This would not be difficult to organise and very much simpler than court hearings elsewhere. If all the surveys had to be done within the year of 1086, this is the best logistical option. It is for this reason that this option is favoured by the writer. In his professional but subjective judgement it is preferred because it is what he would have done if he had been organising the Domesday survey!

The surveys and the giving of evidence do not complete the activities. Little Domesday and the Exeter Book could be consistent with the process of the first editing of the field book type entries found in the ICC. The main important difference is that, for each county, the landholders and tenants are listed at the beginning in a sort of index and the details of the holdings of each tenant are listed. Generally, this is consistent with the view that the prime purpose of the survey was fiscal. However, it is surprising that the fiscal totals are not listed with the initial list of tenants and that the tenants are not listed in the order of the size of their holdings (see Appendix F for two examples of lists of tenants and the fiscal size of their holdings). Livestock is still included in the Exeter Book and Little Domesday, although there is no reason to suppose that this information was used directly to determine the tax base. Livestock is absent from the main Domesday survey.

On the evidence of Cambridgeshire and Huntingdonshire in Domesday, particularly those in Armingford and Toseland Hundreds, the survey entries are much clearer and easier to categorise than those in the ICC. It is consistent with a document that has been vigorously edited for a second time and possibly significantly revised where necessary.

Although this sequence is possible, the evidence to support it is limited as the only direct comparisons we have are the Cambridgeshire Hundreds that survive in ICC, compared with those in Domesday and the Exeter Book, with the comparable Domesday counties. We also have the apparently less edited Little Domesday. However, we have no alternative evidence which might suggest any other sequence of events.

6.6 Preparatory stages before the fieldwork

The Domesday survey was a task of considerable political and logistical importance. It is very unlikely that the whole idea was conceived suddenly out of nothing and all the details established at one single 5-day meeting at midwinter 1085. This is not how taxation, legislation and the logistics of property tax revaluations work. Such a timetable would, in the writer's opinion, be impossible. The concept of such a survey must have been thought about and discussed over a long period. They were levying taxes (gelds) on the basis of the Hidage assessments and they would have been aware of the need for a revaluation of the Hidage basis. It is the writer's opinion that there must have been significant comprehensive planning for a survey carried out before the meeting. All the detailed arrangements cannot have been achieved in such a short time. Perhaps the technical aspects of exactly what information was to be gathered had already been determined before the midwinter meeting. Perhaps the Christmas meeting was to establish and agree the political importance of the enterprise. Perhaps the 5-day discussion was about the assignment of responsibilities and logistics and the main responsibilities then assigned for each circuit. It is not otherwise possible to see how all the fieldwork and hearings could have been completed within a year if there had not already been such quite detailed preparatory work.

If we suppose that, at midwinter 1085, the political decision had been made to fire the starting gun and to commence the survey, and the main circuit responsibilities were assigned, there must have been a further period of preparation before work could begin in the field. Thereafter, there would have been the actions required for the appointment of key staff within each circuit and, in turn, the recruitment by them of their work teams and the procurement of the supplies they would require in the field. It would then have been necessary to inform all counties of the survey and the information that would be required of them. The County Reeve or other official would, we might suppose, pass this information on to the Hundreds and the Hundreds to the vills. The County Reeve would presumably have the task of identifying and recruiting those to give evidence. The visiting teams would then have been deployed to their circuits at a travelling pace of perhaps no more than 20 miles (*c.* 32 km) a day, for 6 days in the week. It seems unlikely that that these preparatory works could be completed in less than 3 months, which means that effective work in the field would not begin before April at the earliest, which would conveniently coincide with better weather.

6.7 Logistics of the field surveys

It is not possible to determine with certainty solely from a study of the text of the survey whether the Domesday surveyors visited every vill themselves in 1086 or relied on recent surveys already available to them in that year and then verified and updated the data at hearings in the Hundreds. The writer's view is, as above, that each vill must have to be visited by the surveyors at some time. Perhaps this had happened before the survey commenced as part of the administration of the Hidage system. More likely, in the writer's opinion, a survey similar to ICC was carried out in every county as a preparation for Domesday before 1086.

Is it logistically possible that field surveys were carried in 1086? The sole reason for the widespread supposition that the whole survey was completed from start-to-finish in 1086 – and for the supposition that it was completed in less than 8 months by Lammas 1086 – seems to be the entry in the *Anglo-Saxon Chronicle* for 1085. It describes the Christmas 1085 meeting in Gloucester and says: 'all the recorded particulars were afterwards brought to him' (Ingram and Giles 1847, 124). This appears to be the sole grounds for postulating this impossible shorter timetable. Nevertheless, if each vill was to be visited during the 1086 survey, the time and manpower requirements are significantly larger. Moreover, for this to happen the professional skills must have been immediately available with little further training and all writing materials in stock either held centrally or in the shires. Table 17 seeks to show the manpower required if the field survey was done within about a 7-month period from April to November in 1086.

The calculations suppose that the inspection and the fact gatherings for each vill could be completed in 1 day and there would be a day to transfer to the next vill. This might well be over-optimistic, especially for the larger vills. Inclement weather could also cause delays, even if the survey was conducted in the summer months. These timings in Table 17 are optimistic calculations with the minimum manpower. The logistics show that it might just have been feasible for the rural vills. It is a possible but not a probable scenario. Table 17 takes no account of the work involved for the surveys of the 112 boroughs.

TABLE 17. Minimum manpower and timings for field visits to all vills

	Manors	*Vills*	*Days work per team per vill*	*Days for teams travel between vills*	*Total days*	*Total weeks at 6 working days per week*	*No. teams to complete within 26 weeks*	*No. man/weeks if 6 per team*
A	b	C	d	E	f	g	h	I
Armingford	63	14	1	1	28	5		
Cambridgeshire	446	145	1	1	290	48	2	12
Huntingdonshire	140	90	1	1	180	30	1	6
Essex	900	434	1	1	868	145	6	36
All Domesday	21,000	13,000	1	1	26,000	4333	167	1000

It further supposes, for the sake of this exercise, that each inspection team might have comprised – at the minimum— six persons working 6 days a week. Two of them would be literate and knowledgeable with four support staff such as servants, grooms and porters. The team could hardly be smaller and might have been larger. If Sundays and other holy days and days of illness are taken into account, it is unlikely that the mean per person was more than about 275 working days a year. Thus, according to this scenario, Armingford Hundred could be completed in 5 weeks: a timetable looks to be a reasonable expectation taking into account the nature of the landscape. Nationally, it requires the ambitious mobilisation of at least 1000 men, of whom 400 would be literate and knowledgeable.

There must have been additional people involved in overseeing the task – perhaps on a regional or circuit basis – to ensure consistency of approach and ensuring there were no omissions from Domesday whether through idleness, incompetence or corruption. These are not included in the above estimates.

6.8 Logistics of judicial hearings

It might have been that evidence under oath was only given during visits to the vills and manors. They could have used the existing procedures of the manor courts. This would be a straightforward, feasible method of capturing the data, obtaining opinions of others and enabling the commissioners and their appointed deputies to make the judgements necessary. There might have been no need for further hearings. This appears to the writer the most likely way in which the survey captured the data (see Appendix H).

However, for the purpose of this analysis, let us suppose that the inspections alone do not complete the task and the frequent references to those who gave evidence in the survey indicates that there might have been, in addition, separate hearings of a judicial nature at a central place in each Hundred. Table 18 indicates the manpower required for such a scenario. Those giving evidence would certainly have opinions on matters of title. They might have opinions on other matters but it seems unlikely that they could have made judgements on values or over-ruled the Domesday surveyors.

These calculations suppose that a hearing for each Hundred could be completed in 3 days. This again may well be over-optimistic. Those with a first-hand

TABLE 18. Logistics of judicial hearings

	Vills	Hundreds	Duration of hearing in days	Travel between Hundreds	Total days	Total weeks at 6 working days per week	No. teams required if completed within a 30 weeks period	No. man/ weeks if 20 per team
Armingford	14	1	3	0				
Cambridgeshire	145	16	3	2	96	16		
Huntingdonshire	90	4	3	2	24	4		
Essex	434	23	3	2	138	23		
All Domesday	13,000	600	3	2	3600	600	20	400

knowledge of litigation in courts or at tribunal hearings will know that the legal proceedings take time. There is the gathering and preparation of the evidence before the hearing, the assembling of the persons required on specific days and in the right place, the taking of the oaths and then the judicial hearing itself and the recording the evidence from all witnesses. The writer remembers from first-hand experience that the timescales for the hearings of the UK Lands Tribunal cases (as it then was and now known as the Upper Tribunal of the Lands Chamber) were, in practice, controlled by the speed with which the presiding member wrote his handwritten notes during the proceedings. Similarly, in 1086 the speed of the scribes' quills would no doubt have dictated the pace of the hearings.

The estimates in Tables 17 and 18 are optimistic and test a general belief that some sort of Domesday draft, however partial and incomplete, was ready for presentation to the King (if he was in England much after Lammas 1086) before his death in Normandy. When planning the execution of the survey, those with responsibility would have taken into account the available numbers and competence of the manpower. Nationally, for the scenario in Table 18, the immediate availability of a workforce is required of at least 400 persons of whom 40% would be literate, trained, adequately instructed and knowledgeable, together with adequate supplies in stock. If both the survey and the judicial hearings were carried out in 1086, this required the mobilisation of more than 500 literate persons. These estimates do not include those in supervisory roles, which would have included the checking of the surveyors returns. There would certainly be errors of omission and commission and corruption.

The above estimates do not prove that all the data for all the vills could not have been captured within the year 1086 but then it also does little to support such a timetable. Perhaps the timetables are just feasible and the work was completed in this very short timetable but it is a timescale that an experienced surveyor would be unwise to promise. It leaves no room for anything to go wrong; and things always do go wrong. It is impossible to suppose that there were any meaningful results for the King to see at the Lammas 1086 meeting at Salisbury, although it would have been a good opportunity to monitor progress and re-inforce the political importance of the survey. In view of the logistical obstacles, it seems to the writer that what was presented to the King before his death in September 1087 can, at best, only have been a draft, and probably a partial one at that: and then only if the relevant documents had been transported to him in Normandy.

6.9 The logistics of the editing and production of the written list

A common opinion seems to be that the whole survey was completed within the year of 1086 by means of jury hearings in the counties. The reasons for this view seem to be based on 1086 comments in the *Anglo-Saxon Chronicle* referred to in Section 6.7 above and the addendum at the end of Little Domesday referring to the date 1086 and the naming of the persons giving evidence, particularly in the ICC. It is likely that the valuation date was the circumstances as they were in 1086. As argued above, it is just possible that the data gathering was done in 1086 but only after planning and substantial preparations that must have occurred before December 1085. This timetable is logistically difficult and unlikely but just possible. It is, however, inconceivable that the written record that has survived was completed within that 1-year timetable.

6.10 Modern comparisons

Nowadays, when the data has been captured on computer and ordered in a pre-determined manner, a valuation list the size of Domesday (21,000 entries excluding the boroughs) could be printed and prepared for publication within a day or so. Before the advent of computers the valuation lists for England and Wales – numbering about 25 million entries – were prepared by the Valuation Office (as it then was) on manual or electronic typewriters in about 100 separate local valuation offices. The typing of the lists started about 6 months before the date at which the lists were to be published, although no single person in any of the offices would be working on them exclusively. It should be possible to make a more accurate calculation of the typist time for the production of the valuation lists but, for this purpose, it is estimated that it took about 10 typist/years to type the 25 million property entries in the valuation lists.

6.11 Size of the task

The size of Domesday with 13,000 vills and 21,000 manor entries is very much smaller than those databases described above. One person could manually type a valuation list of 21,000 entries with clear, clean data in no more than 10 working days. But the task of preparing a workable copy of the Domesday Book from the survey records was much more arduous. The data gathered in the field or at judicial hearings was not clear and clean and had to be edited. It is supposed, as above, that the data collected in the field was recorded in a form similar to that now seen in ICC. The next or second version might look like the data as recorded in Little Domesday. The last version is in the format that we now see for all counties in Great Domesday. The above sequence would, in the writer's opinion, require the writing of two draft copies before the last version. That means it is a three-stage process after the collection of all the data with periods in between for the drafts to be checked, and the next stage planned.

6.12 The constraints

The capture of the information in the field, and each edited version of Domesday, was written by quill pen, which is slower than a modern pen and much slower than typing. If the speed of quill pen handwriting were about one-fifth of the speed of typing, then the actual writing of the Domesday Books would have taken about 4 man/years for each stage. It may be that the editing tasks fell to a team of clerks, in which case each stage could be completed in 6 months.

6.13 The calculations

The writer's estimate is that, in total, the tasks of sorting and writing a penultimate draft required 4 man/years of work. The timetable for the task could be proportionally less than 4 years if several scribes were used. However, the general informed opinion, among the restricted number of experts with knowledge of medieval scripts, indicates that a single scribe wrote the final fair copy of Great Domesday. The issue is discussed by Michael Gullick and his opinion is accepted for the purpose of this analysis (Gullick 2003, 151, 153). In which case it would be surprising if the version of Domesday that has survived was available much before the end of year 1088. It might be the case that usable copies in some form, perhaps in parts, were available not long before King Williams' death, written in different hands. and perhaps what we see now is a fair copy made at a later date.

What is certain is that the work of sorting, editing and writing Domesday was a significantly large task. For the planning, the task of editing and writing up the survey data, the most optimistic timetable might be as follows in Tables 19 and 20, and the elapsed time might then be as in Table 20.

6.14 Conclusions about timetable

The results of the analysis are in summary these:

- There must have been substantial thought given to, and preparatory work done for, the survey before the Gloucester meeting in December 1085.

TABLE 19. Volume of work for writing list

	Actions after collection of data in field. Completed December 1086	Duration of task in man/months	Size of team	Elapsed months
1	First drafts re-ordered from a geographic basis to lists of Tenants-in-Chief in each County	48	24	2
2	Second draft correcting errors and revising figures	48	24	4
3	Penultimate drafts for each circuit in different hands	48	24	6
4	Final fair copy in single hand	12	1	18
	Totals	153 months or 16 man/years		Not less than 1½ years or about June 1088

Surveying the Domesday Book

	Actions	No. man/ months	Size of team	Months to complete	Elapsed months after data in field assembled	Estimated completion date	Comments
1	Collection of data in the field (as in Tables 12 and 13).					assumed December 1086	At this stage the information collected might have been in the format seen in ICC
2	Editing and re-ordering from geographic bases to Tenants by counties	210	105	2	2	end February 1087	Assume teams of 3 for each of the 35 counties
3	Assessment of results to date			1	3	end March 1087	Consideration of results of the drafts and planning next stage. These drafts might have been in the format now seen in Little Domesday
4	Editing to correct errors and removal of information not required (such as livestock) and consolidation	105	105	1	4	end April 1087	The editing would change the format from that in Little Domesday to that found in the other counties
5	Assessment of results to date			1	5	end May 1087	Consideration of results of the drafts and planning next stage
6	Writing final fair copy	12	1	12	17	Spring 1088	With some minor editing, writing of the draft that has survived

TABLE 20. Elapsed time

- The detail and consistency of the data in Domesday makes it probable that site inspections took place at some point, either during 1086 or prior to that year.
- It is just feasible that the work of inspections and the judicial hearings could have been carried out in 1086, by December. Such a timetable is very demanding and unlikely.
- The work of editing and making of the fair copy in a single hand would probably require a period of not less than 18 months from the receipt of the data relating to any field surveys and judicial hearings, to a central point (Winchester).
- The final draft of Great Domesday – in a single hand – could not have been available before June 1088.
- King William may have seen work-in-progress but is unlikely to have seen any version of the final draft before his death in 1087.
- There was no complete national final draft because in Little Domesday covering Essex, Suffolk and Norfolk the data were only partly edited.
- The entries for the 112 boroughs are incomplete.

CHAPTER 7

Conclusions

7.1 What did Domesday achieve?

Domesday was essentially a fiscal revaluation of an *ad valorem* property tax valuation list, albeit a radical and successful revaluation. It started with the strong foundation of the existing Hidage assessments and all the associated records and the effective existing machinery that must have been part of this long-established successful tax. This continuity is central for the understanding of Domesday, which could not have been completed without this strong base. Domesday did not arise out of nothing at Christmas 1085. It was a development – possibly after two decades of thought and discussion now lost to us – and founded on a strong and effective, pre-existing system.

The essential structure of each assessment for each manor was:

i)   the Hidage assessment;
ii) the number of ploughlands; and
iii) the assessed value.

The survey did not generally add additional classes of taxpayers, although it no doubt updated the existing list and brought in missing taxpayers. Nor did the survey, in general, add any newly taxable properties, though it may well have added properties that should have been assessed in the Hidage system. The survey did not fundamentally widen the scope of what assets were assessed for tax. The unit of comparison and valuation for Domesday was the ploughland; and the ploughland was in concept either identical, or at least very similar, to the hide. Domesday valuations, like the Hidage assessments, were based on the annual agrarian worth as measured by the amount of arable land which reflected the productive capacity.

Domesday did, however, update the data and add new dimensions. It reviewed the ploughlands and recorded the facts as they were at 1086. Obviously, there had been changes in the previous hundred years and the total number of ploughlands is greater in total in the survey than the number of hides. It created a more precise measurement of the ploughland, no longer banded in groups of five, as was the case for Hidage assessments in Cambridgeshire. It created a national list with acceptable national consistency. It recorded many other facts that were value significant and it also added some additional anomalous categories such as watermills and saltworks. But, most importantly, it added the monetary assessment in the form the annual rental value in 1086. This last new factor was a fundamental change. The Domesday survey successfully created a new, sound and potentially useable tax base even though it was not used.

7.2 Domesday considered in the historic context of taxation

How does the Domesday survey compare with other national British cadastres? The term 'cadastre' is used here to mean 'a register of property to serve as a basis of taxation' and not to describe any property list for any purpose (*Shorter Oxford English Dictionary* 1977). Table 21 shows the outline of the Domesday survey and of four other comparable taxes selected because all of them had nationwide cadastres. The tithe was a significant and enduring tax but is not included in Table 21 because it did not operate from a cadastre. The taxes are listed in the order of their fiscal effectiveness with the most tax-efficient being on the right-hand side of the Table. The Domesday survey is in the left column.

The reasons why some taxes succeed and others do not are complex and this paper only attempts brief descriptions for the purpose of comparison, and to set Domesday in its fiscal context. The 1910 Increment Value Duty was based on a complete and thorough cadastre covering all 10 million real property holdings, recording the entire capital value of each holding including the buildings (if any) and the value of the site only. It was therefore much more broad-based than Domesday. It is, nevertheless, an interesting comparison with Domesday for two reasons. The field surveys were also done rapidly during a 15-month period and it also failed as a tax. The speed of assessment was made logistically possible by four factors. First, the entire country was by then covered by Ordnance Survey 1:2500 maps, which mapped and uniquely identified every land parcel and gave to each of them an area in acres to three decimal places.[1] Second, the task required the formation of an entirely new department, the Inland Revenue Valuation Office, specifically to complete this survey. Thirdly, the Inland Revenue had the experience and the records gained from the administration of Income Tax Schedule A. Fourthly, there was still some institutional memory of the administrative requirements arising from the tithe surveys in the decades after the *Tithe Commutation Act* 1836. Furthermore, travel was facilitated by the railway network. None of these advantages applied to the Domesday survey.

The 1910 tax never collected more than it cost. It failed fiscally because it attempted to tax *betterment* of land: that is the increase in value due to the actions of the state or community rather than the actions of the individual owner.[2] Such a tax was conceptually impossible until the advent of the planning system brought in by *The Town and Country Planning Act* 1947. However, the increment duty assessments continued to be used as a basis for the filing system

---

1 In reality, the field surveys could not be accurate to this degree.
2 The thinking behind this tax was influenced by the works of the American economist Henry George, 1839–1897, particularly *Progress and poverty* (George 1886).

7. Conclusions

Tax	Domesday survey	Increment Value Duty	Land Tax	Hidage assessment (Danegeld)	Rating
Duration	*Assessed 1086*	1910–1915	1692–1963	991–1162	16th century–1990 in its original form
What was assessed	*Probably the arable land*	All real property	All real property and some sources of personal income	Agricultural productivity: probably focused on arable land	All real property until agricultural property was exempted in 1930
How assessed	*Rental value*	Capital value	Annual value	Probably the productive capacity of the arable land	Rental value
Beneficiary body	*Crown*	Central government	Crown/central government	Crown	Local authorities
Who pays	*Tenants-in-chief*	Vendors when property sold	Owners	Tenants-in-chief	Occupiers
Comments	*Never used as a source of taxation*	The tax never yielded more than the cost of assessment and collection; not a fiscal success	An annual tax the revenue from which became less significant over the centuries because the assessments were not revised	An effective tax base yielding significant sums and used initially only in times of national emergency	The main buoyant source of local government revenue for 400 years

TABLE 21. A taxation comparison

in the Inland Revenue Valuation Office for the next 60 years. The writer knows from personal experience that it was a thorough and complete record.

Land Tax was initially a success with a cadastre of an acceptably high standard. It followed on from and, in many ways, resembled the effective 'monthly assessments' commenced in the Commonwealth period of the 17th century. It was also more widely based and more clearly focused than Domesday and was map based. It was therefore a better fiscal instrument than Domesday. But as no revaluations were carried out, it was not buoyant and gradually declined in fiscal importance. As an incidental consequence of the introduction of Pitt's income tax in 1799, it became a redeemable charge on land and took a long time to die.

The UK Rating system, prior to 1990, an *ad valorem* annual property tax, provided a fiscally sound system for centuries and was, in the 1980s, collecting more than 10% of the total national tax receipts, which is a high proportion by international standards. The system prior to 1930 (when agricultural land was exempted) included all real property and thus had a wider scope than Domesday. Prior to the revaluation in 1963, the valuation lists were a local responsibility (i.e. they were undertaken by local councils) and were of variable qualities and lacked a national consistency. In effect, there was no national rating cadastre until the Inland Revenue Valuation Office for England and Wales took on responsibility for the valuations for the 1963 revaluation. Property taxes such as this are buoyant if regular revaluations are carried out and the database is kept up-to-date, and they then respond well to local needs. The updating of property tax lists is a task that requires discipline and resources. It is usually politically contentious. Failure to revalue delays and exacerbates the inevitable political decisions. Domesday would have had to be updated annually or at least regularly if it had been used as a basis for tax.

The Hidage assessment system – Danegeld – must be regarded as a fiscal success because, during its at least 170-year existence, it was able to collect significant amounts of revenue in times of national emergency. That is a fiscal triumph. Although the Hidage assessments were often banded in multiples of five (at least in Cambridgeshire), they must have reflected, however crudely, an ability to pay.[3] It would not otherwise have succeeded as a significant tax over such a long period. One reason for its continuity was that the Hidage cadastre was not denominated in money but in the Hidage unit. In theory, it did not need revision, as the amount of land sufficient to support a family or the amount of land a team of oxen could plough in a year (or whatever was meant by hide) remained the same regardless of inflation. It sufficed for the collection of a quota tax. Even so, such relativities do slowly change over time and revisions were made, for instance, in some Hundreds in Cambridgeshire. Property taxes such as this, for which the bases are not revised, become less effective and eventually become politically unsustainable. This appears to be what happened to the Hidage system for the collection of Danegeld.

The Domesday survey was, in theory when judged as a cadastre, superior to the Hidage system. The underlying database was thorough within its own narrow terms of reference. The assessments were much more precise. The tax base identified and accurately estimated the ability to pay of the land-owning tenants who controlled the major source of the wealth. It was a good cadastre and could have served as a good basis for the collection of a quota tax. One might suppose that it was intended as an improved replacement for the Hidage system.

Why then was it not used as a taxation basis? Why did the Hidage system continue to be used as a taxation base for more than 70 years after Domesday had been completed?

It may well be that the value relativities determined in Domesday between and within counties did have an effect on the allocation of the burden for subsequent quota taxes in subsequent years and even in subsequent centuries. Perhaps this is why the Domesday Books were preserved. However, it seems that no tax was ever directly collected using the individual assessments of the Domesday survey. It therefore seems that this enormously successful and expensive undertaking resulted in no direct fiscal benefit. A study of the text of the Domesday survey alone gives no explanation of why this is so. The following points might be considered when trying to answer this question.

---

3   There are two points to make about the banding into units of five. First, this may indicate a traditional view that this quantity reflects an obligation to supply one fighting man. The second point is to note the parallel with the 'banding' system for the UK Council Tax from 1991.

The final version of Domesday contains too much detail. All the recorded data are relevant for assessment and valuation. The additional data could have been used to clarify the basis of the assessment for taxpayers and avoid dispute about the quantum of assessment, in so far as any such dispute was tolerated under the rule of King William. But, for the collection of taxation, we do not need anything but the taxpayer, the identity of the property and the final value. As the purpose is fiscal there is a surfeit of information included in the final list.

All property lists need periodic revision if they are to be of continuing use as working documents. Agricultural tenures change on average at least once a generation. The physical circumstances, relating to the land, change more slowly especially if, as in Domesday, it is only the underlying land being assessed. But there would nevertheless have been changes. Perhaps more ploughlands were brought into cultivation. Some woodland would have been felled and converted into meadow, pasture or arable. War and natural disasters can affect agrarian productivity. If a property list, be it a taxation cadastre or estate terrier or a land registry, is to be used as a working document it must be kept up-to-date. It is otherwise only an out-of-date historic record of the time it was made. Updating requires continuing manpower resources and almost as much political determination as the original survey; and the more information in the list, the greater the amount of work. Perhaps this determination was lacking after the death of King William and it was politically easier to continue using the Hidage assessments and collect lesser but regular sums. What we have in Domesday is an image of agrarian conditions in 1086. If it had been used for direct taxation it would have been revised as required, in which case the original 1086 document might well not have survived. Thus, our knowledge of history gains from a fiscal failure.

Perhaps Domesday failed fiscally because it was ahead of its time. The history of direct taxation in Britain, particularly in England, can be seen as a long search for bases of assessment that reflected an ability to pay and to identify the assets that create the taxpayers' ability to pay. We now know that, for most direct taxes, more than 80% of the revenue comes from the wealthiest 20% of the taxpayers and it is necessary to focus taxes to take this factor into account. The succession of taxes such as aides and subsidies in the Middle Ages struggled to find an effective basis for taxation. However, generally there was progress made towards more logical bases of assessments more correlated to the ability to pay starting with the monthly assessments during the Commonwealth period and then the annual Land Tax from 1692, and then income tax. There were backward steps to the more regressive capitation or poll taxes in 1377, in the 17th century and in 1990. There were diversions from that path from 1747 onwards to a dozen taxes on domestic establishments, attempting to capture indications of wealth. These included such things as carriages, plate chests, servants and racehorses. The main development came with income tax, first introduced as a temporary measure in 1799. But 700 years earlier, the Domesday survey devised a basis of taxation that closely reflected an ability to pay and it identified those who *could* pay. However, the rich and powerful had the most to lose and, then as now, were the ones most likely to resist a change in assessment that adversely affected them. This incentive to resist change might have been increased because of the exemption of demesne land from the 6s geld was unlikely to persist after the survey. Perhaps this is what happened after the death of King William, who was clearly the prime mover in the project. The Domesday focus was firmly on the rich and powerful who were able to defy a less powerful ruler.

7.3 Narrow focus of Domesday

A first glance at Domesday can give a false impression of a broad and comprehensive list, revealing the entire economy and society in England in 1086. In fact, it does not do so because it has a narrow focus. It is not a complete reflection of English society in 1086 because it is only concerned with the agrarian economy. No doubt agriculture was the major economic activity but it did not constitute 100% of the whole economy nor did it employ 100% of the workforce. The rest of the economy is not directly visible in the survey. There are, of course, many items in Domesday all listed in apparent detail. It records the agricultural workforce, at least in part (see Appendix B), the amount of meadow, the amount of pasture and the extent of woodland grazing, and some of the livestock numbers (in Little Domesday, ICC and partially in the Exeter surveys). All of these are recorded although not, in fact, always completely comprehensively.

We can make a model of the agrarian use of land from the statistics that can be extracted from the survey where we have credible livestock numbers. Of course, as in any model, the results depend on the assumptions (see Appendix C). Almost all these listed items were value-significant factors and are reflected in the monetary assessments. They are relevant to the valuation of the arable land and that was the reason for capturing the data. Domesday, and the agriculture information in the works of Walter of Henley, Bishop Robert Grosseteste and others, allow us a glimpse of agriculture in England in 1086 and the period thereafter (see Appendix A).

There is a much longer list of things that were not recorded because they were not relevant to the purpose of the survey. As discussed above, almost no buildings are recorded because the survey was not concerned with the built environment. Thus, looking at only Domesday, we have little indication of how much urbanisation there was outside the settlements designated as Boroughs. There must have been other small townships or larger villages just as there are in any landscape. They are often invisible or only seen as shadows in the survey.

Although categorised persons are recorded, Domesday is also an incomplete record because even the agricultural workforce must have been at least 5–8 times as large as that recorded. It would otherwise have been impossible to farm the land. It seems possible that the workforce in the Demesne land was not recorded at all. It is no census; not even of those employed in agriculture (see Appendix B).

The livestock listed, at least in the Eastern counties, may be reasonably comprehensive for some categories, but is incomplete for horses and unclear for oxen and the young-stock being reared to replace those working beasts. The livestock listed in Cornwall in the Exeter book does not look in any way to be comprehensive.

Nevertheless, in the *Anglo-Saxon Chronicle* for the year 1085, the writer states:

> So very narrowly indeed, did he commission them to trace it out, that not a single hide, nor yard of land, nay, more-over (it is shameful to tell, though he thought it no shame to do it), not even an ox, nor cow, nor swine was there left, that was not set down in his writ. (Ingram and Gullick 1847, 125)

This is a bit of journalese. It may generally correctly reflect on the thoroughness of the survey in relation to taxpayers and manors, the taxable unit. But it is not accurate in every respect. We really do not know how many oxen there were or how and where replacements for the working teams were bred (see Appendix C). In Cornwall, the data recorded shows no sign of being anything like a comprehensive count of livestock (see Appendix E). In the event, the final version of Domesday (that is all except Little Domesday) does not mention livestock. We might suppose that the livestock numbers, although interesting and helpful in revealing stocking rates, were not essential for the narrow focus of the survey.

7.4 Reflections on value

In summary, these are the conclusions related to value:

- There is evidence that the values recorded represent annual rental values and not rents passing.
- We can be sure that the bases of the survey were the agrarian values.
- We can presume that the values related to the land only as almost nothing related to the built environment is listed.
- We suppose that the ploughland (identical or very similar in concept to the hide) was the unit of comparison and the unit of valuation.
- We may believe that all other assets recorded related to, and influenced, the value of the arable land.

Nevertheless, we still have no clear idea how the surveyors progressed from the assessment of the ploughlands to a 1086 valuation figure. The reason for this is that we do not know how the surveyors assessed the quality of the land and other value-significant assets, rather than numbers and extent of these assets.

7.5 Reflections on the logistics and timetable

We can be certain that the Domesday survey was not suddenly conceived out of nothing in a single meeting at Christmas 1085 and then subsequently a fully completed survey was presented to the King before he left for Normandy for the last time in autumn 1086. It cannot have happened so fast. Indeed, it is logistically impossible for the King to have been shown the final fair copy version of Domesday that we now have before his death in September 1087. It is unlikely that he could have seen even a draft version unless the documents were transported to him in Normandy.

Almost all taxes are developments of previous taxes. We can see this repeatedly in later examples, thus, the Monthly Assessments of the Commonwealth period (and later years) led to the Land Tax in 1692 which, in turn, led on to Income Tax in 1799. In France, the Napoleonic cadastres were preceded by the *taille réele* of the *Ancien Régime* which, in turn, had their roots in more ancient property-based taxes. Even new-concept taxes such as the ill-fated Community Charge of 1990 (1989 in Scotland), a poll tax, took more than 10 years to develop from political concept into law. The Domesday survey had an ancestry. It was the son of the Hidage system of assessment.

The 1085 winter meeting clearly fired the starting gun for the Domesday survey to begin. However, there must have been much thought, preparation, planning and preliminary work carried out for such a survey over months, if not years or even decades, before that date. Planning for an enterprise of this magnitude takes time and, certainly, more than just a few days at Christmas 1085.

Although Domesday was built on the well-established Hidage assessments, the survey required at least 400 man/years work, or possibly as much as 1000 man-years if all manors were visited in 1086. The manors must have been visited at some point, although this might have been before the 1086 survey. The deployment in the field of such a battalion-sized workforce could, with difficulty, have been achieved between Christmas 1085 and (say) April 1086. It might have been just possible to complete a field survey and the hearings by the end of 1086.

The work did not end there. Considerable editing and re-ordering were required. This editing was never completed for Little Domesday. This work has demonstrated that the earliest date that the final draft of Domesday could have been completed – in the form that has survived – is in the spring of 1088. Thus, from start to finish the process took about three years. This timetable accords with the writer's half-century experience of carrying out revaluations for property tax.

7.6 Final summary

This investigation provides a cohesive description of how the Domesday survey was probably carried out. The analyses in this work show the limited focus of Domesday. The survey generally records what was needed for the fiscal purpose. The absence or scarcity of data in Domesday about aspects such as agricultural working populations, agricultural buildings, the built environment or the entire non-agrarian economy is no indication that such an absence or scarcity existed in 1086, or that these matters were not of social and economic importance.

7. Conclusions

As a result, Domesday gives only a partial but focused view of society and the economy. Domesday is a remarkable source of information for the historian but must be used with an appreciation of its purpose and limitations.

The main points from the analysis are these:

1. The purpose was clearly fiscal. Such a successful enterprise must have had one clear single purpose. Multi-purpose property lists of this scale are unlikely to succeed and Domesday was an administrative success.
2. It is well-established that Domesday was principally an agrarian list. The survey was not concerned with the built-environment and is related to the land only.
3. The unit of assessment, the means of comparison, and the unit of valuation was the ploughland. The other listed items are those that influenced the level of value applied to the ploughlands.
4. The dimension missing from Domesday is the quality of the listed items. This gap particularly applies to the quality of the agricultural land. Without this dimension, any mathematical analyses, such as multiple regression analyses, will be incomplete.
5. Domesday cannot be understood without an appreciation of the Hidage/geld assessments. The test of success for a tax is how much revenue it collects in comparison with its cost and how long it endures. By those criteria, the Hidage system of assessment for geld taxation was therefore a remarkable success.
6. The creation and completion of Domesday was only possible because it was a development following on from the well-established, successful and sophisticated Hidage assessments. It was a revaluation with an important added dimension: the rental values.
7. The definition of a ploughland, a fiscal measure, was similar – or identical – to that of the hide.
8. The taxpayers (the tenants-in-chief) and the taxable properties (the manor in a named vill) were those used in the Hidage geld assessments; but brought up-to-date where necessary.
9. We have no comprehensive and precise definition of the concept of a 'hide' although the term clearly did have an exact meaning. Consequently, the exact meaning of a 'ploughland' is not known to us. This impedes a full analysis of Domesday.
10. At some point, all the manors and vills must have been visited and surveyed. This might have been in 1086 or it might have been carried out before that date. It would not have been possible to collect the extensive amount of information and make valuation judgments based only the opinions expressed at judicial hearings.
11. The surveys of the 112 boroughs looked at rents/taxes passing and not rental values. The main determining factor of value was the number of dwelling sites. The borough surveys that we have are incomplete.

12. The whole survey process – from conception to completion – will have taken at least 3 years. It is likely that the process started years, or even decades, before Christmas 1085 and that the final draft was not completed until after the death of King William I in September 1087. The suggestion that the whole work was completed within the calendar year of 1086 is not logistically credible.
13. The Domesday Book was an outstanding administrative success as a survey. It was, nevertheless, a fiscal failure because no revenue was directly collected using Domesday as a tax base.
14. If it had been used a working tax document, it would have been continually updated; and the original would probably not have survived. Thus, historical knowledge benefits from a fiscal failure.

APPENDIX A

Agricultural and estate management in the 11th century

The purpose of this Appendix is to examine the agricultural knowledge and skills exercised by the farmers, bailiffs, seneschals and landowners in the 11th century, in order to better understand the tasks of the Domesday surveyors and the agrarian context in which they did their work.

The data here is mainly gained from four later works by:

1) Walter of Henley, probably written in the 13th century;
2) Bishop Robert Grosseteste, born 1175 and died 1253;
3) The 'Seneschals', undated and anonymous; and
4) 'Husbandry', undated and anonymous.

(All four published in parallel texts in Lamond and Cunningham 1890)

Although all post-date the Domesday survey, it is supposed that the rate of change was slow in those two centuries and the agrarian circumstances were much the same in 1086. All works were widely copied in the medieval period and clearly the practical advice was thought to be of value. They are comparable to the Roman works of Cato and Columella, and perhaps the authors of these later works derived something from them (Ash 1947; Dalby 2010).

There are common factors in all works. First, all are written in the medieval French in use in England at that time. Second, all four books are, in character, agricultural and estate management textbooks, although much more the former than the latter. They are thereby expositions of the best practice. Best practice was, we might guess, not universal. Third, all four are focused mainly on the land farmed in-hand rather than the let land. It should not, from that content, be assumed that the main source of revenue was from land farmed in-hand in the manors.[1] We know from Domesday that in the Armingford Hundred there were 45 ploughs on the in-hand land out of a total of 183 ploughs in the Hundred: that is 25%. Random sampling suggests that it is, overall, much less than 30% of the ploughs were on the in-hand land.[2] We might guess that 60–80% of

---

1 The introduction to Lamond and Cunningham (1890, xi) assumes that the revenue from the in-hand land was important. Other commentators also put too much emphasis on the in-hand land.
2 Random sampling of 30 manors in great Domesday suggests that only 22% of the ploughs were on the in-hand land. But the exact interpretation of some entries is not clear.

the estate revenues came from the rents either from sub-tenants of the manors or from rents and labour from the peasant farmers.

These four works do not cover the management of the let land except insofar as some of the labour obligations to the in-hand land are concerned. All four works make it clear how much attention to detail is required when the land is farmed in-hand. Not all owners were in a position to do so. Not all home farms would have made surplus money. However, the farming of some in-hand land would have given a useful insight into the profitability of the let farms and the affordable rents. Rents are hardly mentioned in any of the four works.

We can obtain revealing glimpses of many aspects of farming practice and farming knowledge in the 13th century and a selection of them are listed below. Most of the practices described will be familiar to farmers of today, especially the older generation.

Management structure

From the Tenant-in-chief, or sub-tenant of the manor, the responsibility first flowed to the seneschal,[3] whose duties correspond quite well to those of a present-day land agent or factor. He was required to know agriculture and to know the law and how to measure land. It seems likely that he was responsible for the management of the let land in addition to the overall supervision of the farming of the in-hand land.

For the farms managed directly, responsibility then was devolved to bailiffs, whose responsibilities corresponded to a modern farm manager. It is required by the treatise on the seneschal that the bailiff be a good husbandman.

The office of the provost does not directly equate to any modern office and it is not clear how it fitted with the management structure. It clearly had a function in the feudal system.

The duties of the hayward include wide supervisory powers. The role was similar to that of a farm foreman. There is surprisingly little in the treatises about the conduct of the hay harvest, important though this must have been.

Labour duties

There are detailed passages on the duties of various specialist agricultural employees. These include ploughmen, waggoners, cowherds, swineherds, shepherds and dairymaids. We might suppose, from the way in which the duties are described, that most or all these posts for the in-hand land were filled by employees rather than those owing day labour to the manor by way of their tenure.

---

3   This term is not used in Domesday. However, such an office must have existed whatever it was called.

Agricultural buildings

There are agricultural buildings actually named in the texts or referred to in passing. The medieval French word *graunge* or *grange* is translated by Lamond as 'grange'. This is misleading and a better translation would be granary. These might have been barns with threshing floors. It is difficult to thresh in the open air in England. Perhaps some were small, closed barns supported on raised mushroom-shaped posts to impede the access by rodents. This granary building was clearly a key building for the arable land. There are dairies (French: *dearie*) in which the milk is stored and butter and cheese are made. There is reference to cow houses. There is mention of dovecots (French: *columbers*). We see that there were stables to house the working oxen and horses, at least on some farms. Sheep were occasionally housed. Not all farms would have had all these buildings. Some would have been much less well equipped. The villeins might often have no more than a longhouse in which to accommodate all their agricultural activities. Overall, it appears there were some farmsteads with all the necessary buildings with which to farm the land.[4]

Estate terriers

Bishop Robert's second rule (Lamond and Cunningham 1890, 123) is an instruction on the creation of an estate terrier (although this term is not used). The categories for each manor are:

i) actual ploughs,
ii) potential ploughs,
iii) amount of arable land in acres,
iv) meadow,
v) pasture for sheep and cows, and
vi) various details about movables including livestock.

This list is not unlike Domesday, in some respects, which is not surprising as it post-dated Domesday. But, unlike Domesday, it does not deal with values. It is a management tool and not a valuation list.

Working the arable land

We can see from the entries that the sequence for arable cultivation was much as might be expected:

i) ploughing,
ii) broadcasting the seed on to (narrow) furrows immediately,

---

4 The Romans built sophisticated and well-designed farm buildings. Vitruvius describes the design of a farmstead in Chapter vi that might be compared with Victorian 'model' farms (trans. Morgan 1914, 183). Cato at chapter 3 in *De agricultura* also contains guidance on the design of farm buildings (Dalby 2010, 61).

iii) harrowing (or maybe secondary ploughing) to cover the seed,
iv) weeding in spring and summer, then at harvest
v) reaping,
vi) binding,
vii) putting in stooks,
viii) carting,
ix) stacking in thatched ricks,
x) threshing, and
xi) winnowing.

All these activities are mentioned. The sequence is much as would be done for the next 800 years until the invention of the seed drill in the early 18th century when a seed bed would have been prepared before sowing. They practised a 2- or 3-year system of crop rotation and the fallow year was important. There are many entries that make it clear that they knew the importance of manure and the need to care for the soil.

There are occasional entries that cause doubts. There is a substantial passage that argues that one ox (or horse) team can plough 180 acres each year (see Walter of Henley cited in Lamond and Cunningham 1890, 9). The carefully worked figures bear no relation to reality and take no account of the days when the weather and the state of the soil make it impossible to get onto the land. There is no allowance that takes into account that most of the ploughing has to be done in confined periods in autumn and spring. It is also well established that oxen are slower than horses and will seldom plough as much as 1 acre a day.[5] Such blatant over-optimism for such a basic operation as ploughing might raise a general question about how far these treatises are aspirational ambitions rather than realistic optimum figures.

Arable crop yields

In the treatise on 'Husbandry', there is a list of seed multiplication for different crops. (Lamond and Cunningham 1890, 71) They are barley × 8, rye × 7, peas and beans × 6, wheat × 5 and oats × 4. However, we might guess these are optimal yields in good years. These figures contrast with those which suggest that 2 bushels of seed an acre yields 6 bushels: a multiplication rate of three. Perhaps this was a more realistic average allowing for failures and adverse conditions. Farmers the world over tend to make optimistic calculations of their crop yields.

---

5   Oxen were slower paced and generally it is thought that they ploughed at 70% or 80% of the speed of a horse team. However, oxen were stronger than the draft horses in the 11th century. There is one passage that states that oxen are more powerful than horses and will keep going in hard conditions that stop horses.

Management of livestock

The husbandry treatises list the gestation periods of animals rounded in weeks. They are all accurate to within 5 days of modern reckonings. It is stated at one entry that a sow can farrow no more than five times in 2 years (in another even more optimistic entry, it suggests three litters per year, although a realistic modern target is 2.3 per year; Nix 2019, 94). Such an outcome is unlikely but it does suggest that they knew the advantages of early weaning.[6] It appears that the swine spent much time in the woods where they could largely fend for themselves. There is mention of folding sheep on the fallow and clearly they appreciated the value of manure on the land.

Measuring land

There is an interesting passage in 'husbandry' on the regional variations in the size of a perch. The most common norm was 16½ ft but, in some regions, it was 18 ft. The variation in this basic measure is shown to vary the size of an acre. The significance of the passage is that it demonstrates that they clearly had the routine land surveying expertise to measure at least to an accuracy of 1 acre and that there were regional variations.

The overall impression of 13th century farming gained from these treatises is that there existed a sophisticated, quantified, financial knowledge of agriculture, at least for some of those involved. It describes an entirely recognisable system of agriculture. Perhaps this should not be a surprise as agriculture had the benefit of experience over millennia. These four treatises can be compared with Cato's *De agricultura* written in about 20 BC, which is also a textbook on the practice of agriculture in the region to the south of Rome (Dalby 2010). Perhaps Bishop Robert had read Cato's work. In the period when these four works were written it was the agriculture that preceded the enclosures but, nevertheless, there is little reference in the treatises to the use and management of the common land which was an important component of the two and three field system. All those works were probably written before the Black Death and perhaps the passages on the management of labour might have been different in tone after the 14th century.

For the purposes of this work, the issue is whether these treatises also provide a picture of agriculture in 1086 and thus assist in putting Domesday into context and provide a background for the analyses in Appendices B and C. It is not easy to judge how the agrarian circumstances in the 13th century differed from those at 1086 using only the sources of the above four documents compared with Domesday. Domesday is a list of titles, occupiers, land use classifications and values without direct reference to buildings or movables. The four treatises are all practical agricultural textbooks with references to crops, livestock, labour, crop yields and costs, thus are not directly comparable but are complementary.

---

6   Sows come into season 5 days after weaning.

It seems likely that the literacy rate had increased in those 150 years. Generally, the written sources from the 13th century are greater in quantity than those from the 11th. The four treatises all put great store on the recording of figures in writing. Note in particular the duties of the office of the 'auditor' (French: *acunters*; probably better translated as book-keeper). It is not clear that literacy and numeracy skills were so widely available in the 11th century. Perhaps also more land was in-hand in 1086.

It is likely that the agricultural practices in 1086 were very similar to those in the 13th century. The rate of change was slow and Robert Grosseteste was probably writing less than 140 years after Domesday. We know from Domesday that manors could afford to pay a geld based on the Hidage assessments which related to agricultural productivity. Agriculture clearly was not at a subsistence level. The entire national economy was dependant on agriculture. It might therefore be supposed that these treatises provide a reasonably accurate picture of agricultural practices in 1086.

APPENDIX B

Agricultural labour and the Domesday survey

The purpose of this appendix is to relate the persons recorded in the survey to the agricultural landscape in which they were working and consider agricultural labour requirements in 1086. The number of men (and it is supposed that they were almost all men) is recorded in the two Hundreds of Armingford and Clavering in Table 22.

TABLE 22. Domesday recorded numbers for Armingford and Clavering

Hundred	Domesday recorded no.	Acres per man
Armingford	448 men	53
Clavering	171 men	75

Note: these figures are the writer's count

In the first instance, the labour requirements are calculated as the number of adult full-time working farm labourers. It was certainly not possible in medieval times to farm and manage those agricultural and woodland enterprises in those Hundreds, with net areas of respectively 23,600 acres and 12,800 acres, with such labour forces if, as Table 25 below suggests, the land was quite intensively used. Agricultural workforces of those sizes would now be easily sufficient in 2020 but only if the arable areas were organised in optimally-sized agricultural units and with the benefit of large modern machines, herbicides, insecticides and all other modern agricultural facilities.[1]

In the 1950s the agricultural textbooks list a norm of 10 annual man/days per acre for small mixed farms, which equates to 30 acres per man for a year of, say, 300 working days (Watson and More 1956, 847).[2] This level of required

---

[1] For comparison, in 2018 in the UK the gross number of persons employed full- and part-time in agriculture was 477,000 for about 17,000,000 ha (40,000,000 acres). The equivalent full-time number of persons might be about 300,000 which is 100–150 acres per person. The national figures encompass many farming systems from extensive pastoral hill grazing to intensive vegetable production.

[2] The figures quoted in Watson and More (1956) relate to a large survey for 1949/50 of actual labour used. There are ten farming systems and six size categories thus making 60 different figures listed for different farming conditions. The category 'mixed' farming on holdings up to 50 acres would be the best match and this is what

labour confirms the writer's experience in the early 1960s as a trainee land agent when one tied cottage for each 40 acres, in addition to the farmhouse, was considered an optimum for part of a farm's fixed equipment; at least by the writer's then employers (although, by 1970, the figure was revised to a tied cottage per 100 acres). Thus, in the 1950s with agriculture in the state that it was then, the number of agricultural workers required for the agricultural and woodland enterprises of this size might be as shown in Table 23.

TABLE 23. Estimated numbers for Armingford and Clavering as if in 1950s

Hundred	1950 nos	Acres per man
Armingford	800 men	30
Clavering	430 men	30

These numbers already significantly exceed the number of persons listed in Domesday, shown in Table 21, before we make any other adjustments. In the 1950s, although much manual work was still involved in agriculture, the farming was largely mechanised with tractors (many with three-point linkages) and some first generation combines and milking machines and the benefit of many agricultural machines, such as seed drills, introduced in the previous 150 years.

In contrast, medieval agriculture was not mechanised. It relied on animal and human power. Milking was by hand. A much larger agricultural workforce must have been required in 1086. A greater proportion of the population depended on agriculture before the industrial revolution. Perhaps a factor of three might be applicable to the 1950s numbers for the estimation of the required workforces in 1086 for non-mechanical agriculture. In which case the figures might be as shown in Table 24:

TABLE 24. Numbers required for Armingford and Clavering in 1086

Hundred	Domesday estimated nos	Acres per man
Armingford	2300 men	10
Clavering	1300 men	10

The 1086 figures are speculative and not precise.[3] We do not know how much of the land area was unused or little used. The calculations also suppose that

---

is used in this analysis. The labour requirements for dairy farming would generally be more than 20% higher at that date and even more if the labour for processing for butter or cheese making are included. Market gardening and some specialist crops would require more labour. Extensive livestock farming would require about 20% less labour.

3   This level of labour requirements has been discussed with several farmers old enough to have first-hand knowledge of farming during the 1940s. None of them thought that farming in the pre-tractor age could be carried out with any fewer labour requirements than a man (or family labour equivalent) for each 10 acres.

Appendix B. Agricultural labour and the Domesday survey

woodland management required, on average, an equal amount of labour per acre. Woodland management, particularly coppicing, can require a large amount of labour.[4] Furthermore, the woodland was used for grazing and was managed as an integral part of the manor unit. Nevertheless, the quantum of this supposition is questionable.

The labour requirements for livestock are spread over the whole year although not evenly as there are labour requirement peaks. For the arable land there is now, and there always was, a main autumn peak labour requirement and a secondary peak in spring. If the numbers in Table 24 are approximately correct then, at a local level, there would have been about 12 men to a hide or ploughland. If the hide or ploughland includes three arable fields of 40 acres each, during the quarter of the year from about August it would require the 12 men to harvest 80 acres, plough and prepare the seed bed and sow autumn-sown cereals for the 40 acres that had been fallow.[5] In addition, they would have to start the autumn ploughing for the 40-acre field which will be spring-sown cereals. The harvest was a time of back-breaking labour and would then, as in later ages, no doubt have involved all the family.[6] The demanding autumn labour requirements suggest that the figures in Table 24 do not overstate the position.[7]

---

4 The main labour requirements for woodland would have occurred in winter outside the growing season when there was less demand for work in the arable fields. Coppicing was (and still is) labour intensive and there were large areas of coppice woodland. Information from modern coppicers (now using chain saws) is that one man can cut a maximum of 2 acres in a year: in the season from September to about March. Other classes of woodland require less labour.

5 The sequence was to plough, then broadcast the seed-corn on the furrows and then harrow the land. Some contemporary medieval illustrations show men broadcasting on the just-ploughed land.

6 It is possible to approximately quantify some of the harvest labour. According to Walter of Henley's *Husbandry* (Lamond and Cunningham 1890), a man could reap corn and tie the sheaves at the rate of 0.4 acres a day although he expresses it differently. The hard labour of reaping is well described in Anna Karenina (Tolstoy 2004, 293). There was at the same time the labour of putting into stooks. Later there was carting or threshing (Lamont and Cunningham 1890, 69). Thus 80 acres of arable in a hide or ploughland in a 3-course rotation would require 200 man/days for harvesting. If the labour were spread over 20 days, or more than 3 weeks with a 6-day week, this would require the labour of ten men. However, the weather would not always be so convenient and the tasks would often be concentrated in fewer fine days using all the family labour available. During this same period the livestock have also to be cared for.

7 For comparison see also Cato's *De Agricultura*, written about 20 BC in which he prescribes a workforce of 13 for a holding of 144 acres which equates to about 11 acres per person (Dalby 2010, 83). See also Columella book II.XII written in the 1st century AD on work rates for various crops (Boyd 1941, 187, 197). Vineyards and fig cultivations required, and still now require, more labour.

Precision is not important (or even possible) because the Table 24 figures exceed the Domesday recorded numbers by factors of more than five in one case and more than seven in the other. This is a large margin and perhaps representative of the south-eastern parts of England in 1086. They demonstrate that the figures recorded in Domesday cannot represent the total labour force actually working in agriculture and woodland management in those particular Hundreds at that time. It may be, as many others have suggested, that what are recorded are only the heads of households. Perhaps there were on average as many as three persons in each household working the land and this is probably an over-estimate. Even if this is so, and the Domesday figures are then multiplied by three, they are still not adequate to farm the land and manage the woodlands.

A striking contrast can be made between the rural Domesday population of Cambridgeshire, as counted by Darby (1977, 336) of 4868 persons, with the number of agricultural labourers (all those employed in agriculture, young and old of both sexes both full-time and part-time) in the county recorded in the 1861 census at 35,427 persons (ONS 2018).[8] That is 20% of the total population of the county. The totals of persons listed differ by a large margin, a factor of seven, but there are similarities in the circumstances.[9] The size of the county is approximately the same at both dates. In 1861, as was the case in 1086, agriculture relied almost entirely on human and animal power. However, there are also differences. By 1861 there was more arable land, due first to the draining of the fens in the two Ely Hundreds and, secondly, because the amount of arable land in the other Hundreds was probably greater with less fallow (perhaps using the Norfolk 4-course rotation) and, thirdly, because more land had been enclosed and cleared of woodland. All three factors required more labour. On the other hand, by the 19th century there had been significant improvements in agricultural methods. Agriculture was more labour-efficient and productive in 1861 than it was in 1086. There were better implements such as, among others, Jethro Tull's seed drill invented in about the year 1701, McCormick's reaping machine and the Meikle threshing machine. The latter reduced the need for labour, at least in the winter months, and caused the 'Swing' riots of the 1830s. There were larger and faster carthorses selectively bred, replacing the slower oxen. Exact comparisons are therefore difficult. Nevertheless, we know from the Domesday statistics that in the Cambridgeshire Hundreds, excluding the Ely Hundreds, the land was quite intensively used in 1086. This required a certain

---

8   The year 1861 recorded the highest number of agricultural workers in any census.
9   It is possible in some cases to see the same pattern at village level. For instance, in Laxton in Nottinghamshire, the 1911 census records 120 persons engaged in agriculture (including women and youths) compared with 35 persons recorded in Domesday. At both dates most of the arable land (perhaps 700 acres) was farmed in the open field system. In the early 20th century the parish carried livestock of about 130 Grazing Livestock Units (for which see Table 26 below) (Haigh 2015). The circumstances at both dates are therefore, to some extent, comparable.

level of labour to cultivate not only the arable land, which might have amounted to between 40% and 60% of the total area in many non-fenland Hundreds, and also to manage the number of recorded livestock (see Appendix C below and the discussion in Darby (1977, 121, 136). Using the figures above but allowing for some areas of extensive grazing in which the labour requirements are lower, we might guess that, in this county of about 550,000 acres, an agricultural labour force of not less than 20,000 would have been required in 1086.[10]

It appears that the two Hundreds which are analysed are not untypical in pattern and essential elements to large areas of Domesday England. The surface area covered by Domesday is about 28 million acres (Darby 1977, 359). The recorded rural population in Domesday is 268,984 (Darby 1977, 338). This would calculate at more than 100 acres for each recorded agrarian working man. Even allowing for the large areas of devastated waste in some counties, and some areas of extensive grazing, such a figure does not appear credible. Similar calculations to those in Tables 20–22 might tentatively suggest a minimum national *agricultural workforce* of no less than 1 million, but perhaps as high as 2.5 million, in the areas covered by Domesday. This figure is higher than many of the estimates of the entire population.

In addition to the workforce directly engaged in agriculture, some of whom are recorded in Domesday, there were also those in proprietorial or supervisory agricultural roles such landowners, stewards, bailiffs and reeves who do not seem to be listed. Any calculation of the agriculturally employed population relying only on the Domesday figures must be looked at with considerable scepticism. Then, in addition, there are all those persons engaged in occupations other than agriculture. If the medieval population was divided into three groups – those who work, those who fight and those who pray – only one of these groups, i.e. those that work, is covered and even that one only partially. There are then, in addition, the young and the old who are not in the workforce. As has been expressed before by those such as Postan (1993, 30): Domesday is no census.

This analysis does not throw much light on what caused some men to be included in the survey and why others were not listed. Clearly the surveyors had definite rules. The writer's tentative view is that the surveyors listed only the heads of households on the peasant let land and did not include those persons working directly for the Lords of the Manor on their own demesne lands; that is on the in-hand land. It would, in any case, be more difficult to determine the proportion of the demesne staff who were mainly employed in agriculture rather than other duties. The order in which the survey data are laid out, with a first reference to the ploughs in demesne, then other ploughs and then the

---

10 There was also the urban population in Cambridge in 1086. There were 373 houses/house plots excluding those listed as derelict (the writer's own count). This could indicate a town population there of 2500–3700. There were, we might suppose, also others not engaged in agriculture in smaller urban areas not designated as boroughs and therefore hardly visible in Domesday, and in monasteries and other religious establishments.

men of various categories, gives some credence to this theory. It might be that only those listed were, in effect, those heads of households tied to the land by the feudal system. If this were so, then the manpower numbers in Domesday make more sense, although the figures throw little light on the size of the total agricultural workforce and still less light on the total population.

APPENDIX C

Agriculture, livestock and land use

The purpose of this appendix is to model agrarian land use in 1086. In two of the sample areas, one in the Little Domesday and the other in Great Domesday but also in the ICC survey, we have data relating to livestock. Analyses are made here in Table 25 of the Armingford Hundred and the Clavering half Hundred.

TABLE 25. The basic figures for livestock and land use in Armingford and Clavering

	Armingford from ICC	Clavering half Hundred in Little Domesday
Area in acres	29,454	16,069
Vills	14	11
Entries	52	19
Hides	104	53
Potential plough	169	81
Grazing livestock units (GLUs)	741	254
Values	£153	£95

Livestock numbers are not recorded in every manor so there may have been under- recording for some reason. Perhaps some livestock were sometimes just not counted.[1] Domesday gives no indication. However, for the purpose of this analysis only the recorded figures are used in the model. In both these areas we have records of livestock and these include cattle, sheep, pigs, goats and horses. Each species requires different areas of land for maintenance and production. In order to make comparisons, each category has been converted to Grazing Livestock Units (GLU), roughly in accordance with the ratios in *The John Nix Farm Management Pocketbook* (Redmond 2018, 85), and shown in Table 26.

---

[1] There are many uncertainties in the recording of livestock numbers in Domesday. The numbers would have been constantly varying over time and seasons with births, deaths and sales. We do not know the conventions that might have applied at Domesday. For instance, with sheep, it is now not uncommon to describe the size of flock by the number of ewes which reflects the productive size, without reference to the number of rams, wethers and lambs at foot. Perhaps Domesday used such conventions.

TABLE 26. GLU Ratios

Cattle	1
Pigs	0.44
Sheep	0.11
Goats	0.2
Horses	0.8

These are approximations because not all cattle equate to one GLU, which is the figure that would apply to a lactating milking cow. Dry cows and beef stores and young stock require less. The same considerations apply to other farm animals. The purpose here is to use GLUs as a means of equating and comparing the different species of farm animals. The figures for pigs are difficult because although they do graze, they are omnivores.

With modern agricultural methods, bought-in feed, productive leys and the application of artificial fertilisers, stocking rates of one GLU per acre on good land are achievable, if unusual. In 1086, without such advantages, the ratio might be 3 or 4 acres of pasture and meadow per GLU at best. The arable fallow would have provided less productive grazing. In woodland, the ratio would certainly have been considerably less productive and very seasonal, even for pigs. An average overall stocking rate of 5 acres per GLU is used hereafter for the calculations.

> **Box 7. Stocking rates on unimproved land**
>
> For stocking rates of unimproved land, compare the now uninhabited island of Stroma in the Orkneys where about 17 feral cattle, including young stock, have survived without any human intervention on 375 acres for the last 40 years. This equates to about 22 acres per head in quite a harsh environment. In Chillingham Park in Northumberland, for more than 500 years, up to 100 head of feral cattle have lived in a 360-acre enclosed park (info. from Chillingham Park, pers. comm.. However, they are fed supplementary food in winter. The stocking rate of 3.6 acres per head would presumably otherwise be markedly different. In the harsh winter of 1947 the number of cattle there dropped to only 13.

Oxen

There is one significant class of livestock that is not directly included in the GLU figures in Table 26. The recording of cattle seems to be inconsistent. Very few of the listed animals in Little Domesday or ICC could have been draft animals. In many manors there are certainly no draft animals listed, although oxen are clearly included implicitly in the plough-teams.

It seems probable that the term 'ploughland' simply represented a formal, mainly fiscal, measure of land. It clearly has some relationship to the presence of the plough (the actual instrument) and some oxen to draw it. It seems probably that it was commonly 120 acres, or 15 acres per ox.[2] There is an occasional entry that indicates a physical presence of the oxen was relevant to the survey. For instance, in Essex there are two entries in Witham and Hatfield Broad Oak in which the numbers of ploughs are recorded as being reduced due to cattle plague (Morris 1983, 1.2, 1.3). Although these are only two such entries (of which the writer is aware), it implies that, normally, when a plough/ploughland is mentioned, there were at least some oxen there. There are many other entries where it seems to be stated that the plough, that is the implement itself, is not there. Does this mean that the plough – and also oxen – were absent?

Whatever the entries recording plough-teams may mean exactly, there must have been draft oxen to pull them. It is generally assumed that the plough-team, at least fiscally, consisted of eight oxen and this is confirmed by very many references to partial teams of two, four or six oxen. This is the case in Cambridgeshire, but there were teams of six and ten in other parts of the country in the 12th century (Lennard 1960). Although it does not affect the calculations we might also suppose that in a hide of 120 acres with a 3-field system, the 40 acres of fallow were not ploughed. The ploughing of the 80 acres of arable with oxen would have taken 90–120 days each year, depending on the soil.

However, in practice, it would seem very unlikely that they would actually plough with a team of eight oxen. No contemporary illustration seems to exist that shows more than four oxen ploughing (see Fig. 3). There is no mention of an eight-team ploughing (known to the writer) other than one of disapproval by Young in the 19th century when in the Chepstow, Newport and Gloucestershire area, where he writes: 'yet the ridiculous custom of ploughing with six or even eight oxen continued here yet never did above an acre a day and very frequently not above half an acre' (Young 1768, 115).

A table compiled by Young also shows how much variation there was in the 18th century in the size of the teams used for ploughing and the daily acreage achieved. Such regional variations no doubt also existed in the 11th century (Young 1768, 237). Confirmation of this can still be seen in the fields of Southeast Asia with one or two cattle or water buffalos pulling ploughs. Eight oxen are not required for ploughing because that amount of power is not needed. Still less power is required for other types of work such as harrowing. One ox can draw a plough but tires more quickly than a team of two or four. It is supposed that these ploughs were generally wheeled ploughs with coulters, ploughshares and mould-boards. There are contemporaneous illustrations which clearly show such ploughs and they are remarkably similar to the horse ploughs still seen

---

[2] For a Roman comparison, see Cato's *De Agricultura* x which specifies for his notional 144 acre farm six oxen, which is 24 acres per ox (cited in Dalby 2010, 83).

today at any ploughing competition. However, there were no doubt many variations, some with mould-boards and with wheels, some with mould-boards but without wheels (*caruca*) and even some ards (*arata*), still used.

We do not know the depth of the average furrow and this affects the power needed, as does the type of soil.[3] Two or four oxen would seem a more practical plough-team as they would have had sufficient drawing power and still be relatively easy to turn in the headlands. Managing a span of eight oxen is difficult and time-consuming. Turning a team of eight at the end of a furrow is awkward and requires sufficient space; and the maps of pre-enclosure fields do not show evidence of open fields having headlands wide enough to do so. The difficulties of turning must have been a consideration because the ploughing of an acre of land in a furlong strip would require about 70 turns of the plough.[4] Perhaps the norm was to use a team of two or four in the morning and another set in the afternoon. Oxen being ruminants they need time to graze and chew the cud. Perhaps teams of four were used on alternate days allowing recovery time. Perhaps the team of eight allowed for some of the oxen being temporarily unsound. No doubt there were rare occasions, when very heavy loads had to be moved, that they yoked a span of eight or more oxen. We know this was the case in South Africa, Southern Rhodesia and Nyasaland (as they were then called) at the beginning of the 20th century, when spans of 30 oxen were required to pull loaded wagons up the long steep rift valley berg (Fitzpatrick 1941, 223: 239).

However, the oxen might have been worked on a day-to-day basis; if the norm was to keep eight mature beasts per plough this would require an additional number of young followers growing on to replace the wastage in the working teams. In dairy herds, where replacements are home reared, it is common to allow for an additional one-third in numbers.[5] In round numbers, this might amount to ten GLUs per recorded plough. Of course, the replacement draft oxen might not have been always home reared. Perhaps it was the norm to import them from other parts of the country with more grazing, such as the Fens. This would make economic sense. The parts of Domesday studied in this work find nothing to help examine this possibility although there was grazing in the Fens (Oosthuizen 2013).

---

3   In years gone by when farmers could remember working with horses, they commonly referred in casual conversation to the lightness or heaviness of land by calling it 'one-horse land' or 'two-horse land' or occasionally 'three-horse land'.
4   This number assumes that the width of a furrow is slightly less than 1 ft (30 cm).
5   We do not know for certain the average working life of an ox in the 11th century or at what age they were put into the yoke; but probably at 4 years old. The length of their working life would have depended on how hard they were worked and how well they were cared for. It is unlikely that the working life averaged more than 5 years at best. For comparison, very high yielding dairy cows now usually last only about three lactations. Mail coach horses in the 18th century seldom lasted more than 2 years in that work.

However the numbers are counted, it is apparent that the non-draft oxen GLU figures listed above in the surveys represent only a fraction, perhaps one-third, of the livestock that must have existed in the two areas examined.

In summary, for the purposes of the analysis in this book, it is supposed that:

i) ploughland was primarily a formal fiscal measure of arable land for a plough-team,
ii) the listings of plough-teams included, in principle, both the plough itself, the necessary yokes, harness, tack and other equipment, and the eight mature oxen needed for the team and the young stock followers.

However, this optimum was probably often not perfectly achieved. Perhaps the surveyors only reduced the number of plough-teams or ploughlands when:

a) the actual plough, the instrument, was not there,
b) the area of land was less than was sufficient for one plough or,
c) there was a clear absence of sufficient oxen to work the land.

This topic has also been considered by others including Fitzherbert (1882), Richardson (1942) and Langdon (1986). It may be that the following extract from the *Anglo-Saxon Chronicle* for 1085 is somewhat misleading, at least in relation to oxen:

> How many hundreds of hides were in the shire, what land the king himself had, and what stock upon the land; or what dues he ought to have by the year from the shire.
> What, or how much each man had, who was the occupier of the land in England, either in land or in stock, and how much money it were worth.
> So very narrowly indeed, did he commission them to trace it out, that not a single hide, nor yard of land, nay, more-over (it is shameful to tell, though he thought it no shame to do it), not even an ox, nor cow, nor swine was there left, that was not set down in his writ. All the recorded particulars were afterwards brought to him. (Ingram and Giles 1847, 125)

In fact, if the quotation is referring to Domesday, not every ox was listed and nor do we really know the total number of oxen. The count of livestock in the Liber Exoniensis is clearly questionable (see Appendix D).

Horses

There are fewer horses recorded in the survey than might be expected and they are not listed consistently.[6] For instance, in Cambridgeshire, Darby, presumably from ICC, records only 212 (including 24 wild mares and seven foals) of which 16 horses are in all 14 vills in Armingford and that is less than one per manor (Derby 1977, 164). In Essex, there are 820 horses including 103 foals, of which

---

6 Some commentators use the term 'rouncey'. This term referred to a riding horse. Draught horses were 'avers' in Middle English. These are archaic terms not now in use in the horse world and so is not used in this work.

only 15 horses and four foals were in the Clavering half Hundred (Darby 1977, 164). The numbers are also from writer's own count for the Hundreds. It seems likely that only those in the hands of the villagers used directly for agricultural purpose and breeding stock are included in Little Domesday or ICC listings. However, it also seems unlikely the young stock (that is foals, yearlings and 2 year olds) are fully and consistently listed.

Those used for transport (human and freight), hunting and military purposes appear to be absent from the survey. We might suppose that horses were not put into work until 3 or 4 years old. Mature working horses and young stock to replace them must have existed in considerable numbers. It might be supposed that such non-agricultural horses were mostly in the demesne ownership of the manors rather than with the tenants. It seems probable from illustrations and other evidence that the horses were smaller than most present-day riding horses, perhaps about 14 hands (about 1.4m), and as hardy as modern native ponies.[7] Nevertheless, these non-agricultural horses would have required significant amounts of grazing and meadow for winter keep and grain in some circumstances when in work. They would have required land to support them. The numbers in Table 27 do not take into account those missing horses.

Land use

Table 27 shows how the land might have been used in 1086 by analysing and comparing Armingford, using the livestock numbers from the ICC, with the half Hundred of Clavering, counting the livestock in Little Domesday.

Of course, not all these assumptions would have been universally correct for every manor. Not all manors would have operated a 3-field system. Some would have used a 2- field system and some not an open-field system.

A comparison can be made between the totals in rows 3 and 12 of Table 27; the figures for which are estimated in different ways and arrive at different, but comparable, figures. There has been no attempt to reconcile the two figures and

---

7   It is likely that the average size of a horse in Britain has increased markedly mainly over the last 150 years. However, there was concern about the size of horses well before that period when a Statute in 1521/22 'An Act concerning horses of higher Stature' (13 Henry VIII c 13) tried to ensure all stallions on common ground were above 15 hands (about 1.5 m). Thoroughbreds are known to be, on average, about one hand higher now, that is about 16 hands (about 1.6 m), than they were in 1860. The original 18th century three foundation 'Arab' stallions, from which all thoroughbreds are descended, were no more than 15 hands Anecdotal documentary evidence suggests Suffolk Punches were about 15 hands at the end of the 18th century. It seems very unlikely that large draught horses, such as the shire, had been developed in the 11th century. Some commentators link the improvement in horse breeding to the enclosures which allowed better control of the breeding stock. Thus, larger draught horses were developed replacing the slower oxen on farms. Perhaps the average medieval riding horse was similar in size and constitution to the horses now seen in Mongolia which are usually about 14 hands high (about 1.4 m).

Appendix C. Agriculture, livestock and land use 133

	A	B	C	D
	FIRST CALCULATION	Unit	ARMINGFORD Hundred	CLAVERING half Hundred
1	Gross parish areas (rounded)	Acres	29,500	16,000
2	Subtract area used for houses, other buildings, waste and other non-agricultural and non-woodland uses. Say 20%	Acres	5900	3200
3	NET PRODUCTIVE AREA	Acres	23,600	12,800
	SECOND CALCULATION			
4	Actual plough-teams	Plough-team	146	81
5	Potential plough-teams	Plough-team	169	90
6	GLUs recorded in survey	GLU	741	254
7	Add draft oxen and followers at 10 GLUs per actual plough-team in row 4	Oxen	1460	810
8	GLUs including draft oxen	GLU	2201	1064
9	Required grazing and meadow as if 5 acres per GLU. Includes arable fallow and woodland grazing	Acres	*11,005*	*5320*
10	Arable area as if plough-teams equate to 120 acres	Acres	17,520	9720
11	Add back two thirds of arable ploughed each year. One-third fallow is recorded in row 9 as grazing	Acres	*11,680*	*6480*
12	TOTAL AGRICULTURAL AREA AS CALCULATED USING GLUs & ARABLE AREA. (both totals shown in italics in rows 9 and 11)	Acres	22,685	11,800

Notes on rows:
Row 1. Areas mainly those in the tables on the 6 in to 1 mile (1:10,650) OS maps of the mid-1800s. The figures are rounded.
Row 2. An estimate.
Row 4. An area of 120 acres of arable, the ploughland, is assumed for these calculations; and assumed to be the same as a hide. This would not invariably be the case.
Row 6. See calculations in paragraph 24.
Row 7. See comments in paragraph above.
Row 9. The number of 5 acres per GLU is an estimate.
Row 11. The model supposes a three field and therefore a three-course rotation for the arable.

TABLE 27. Calculations of land use for Armingford and Clavering

they lie where they fall. Perhaps the non-agricultural and non-woodland areas of the land in row 2 were greater than 20%. The closeness of the two methods does not indicate that degree of accuracy. There are too many uncertain estimated variables. Nevertheless, the totals are close enough to suggest that the calculations provide a rough guide to the 1086 land use and the livestock carrying capacities in those two areas.

The number of oxen is a key figure in the calculations. If the numbers are correct in row 8 of Table 27, large areas of land were needed for their maintenance and production of the oxen. If there were, in reality, fewer oxen, the resulting figures in row 12 would be different. This might have been the case; and a span of eight oxen was probably more a fiscal measure than the actual number of beasts. It might be that the measure of eight oxen to the plough included, say, four mature oxen and the cattle to replace them. The cattle would then have been triple-purpose: draft, milk and meat. Specialised purpose-specific breeding did not commence much before the 18th century. The calculations also assume that sustenance was all from grass; grazing and hay. This was probably largely the case, but it is quite likely they were also fed cereals, mainly oats, which would have reduced marginally the need for grazing. However, draft oxen must have existed in significant numbers and any over-counting in the above figures would be more than off-set by the absence of any non-agricultural horses in the calculations.

The figures also illustrate that, before the use of fossil fuels in agriculture, the amount of grazing and other agricultural resources required to feed and maintain the draft agricultural animals was a substantial part of the gross total agricultural output. (This point is not new. Many others have noted it.)

The calculations suggest that:

i) The areas of grazing land and meadow and woodland grazing were crucial and potentially limiting factors for agricultural production,
ii) the livestock numbers are getting close to the comfortable carrying capacity of the lands in use for agriculture or woodland,
iii) there might have been more land that could have been brought into productive use, and
iv) that the livestock numbers in the survey in the Hundreds under discussion included both the demesne and the tenants' animals as there was not enough grazing or meadow to support much more.

The model gives an insight into land use and agricultural conditions in the two Hundreds discussed here. A model such as this can only serve as a general indication and depends on the assumptions made, and these are stated above. Different assumptions will result in different figures but would still broadly support the four conclusions above; particularly the first. This is the most important insight in this analysis of land use in 1086. It stands on two firm foundations. The grazing and forage requirements for grazing animals are known and we can relate them to the known areas being analysed. The importance of the grazing capacity broadly accords with Rackham's calculation using different but comparable figures relating to the whole area covered by Domesday (Rackham,1986, 335–6).

In summary, the agricultural land listed in Domesday seems to have been quite intensively farmed, although not to its absolute maximum capacity.

APPENDIX D

Landholders and totals

The purpose of this appendix is to examine the potential tax implications for the taxpayers in two counties. The compilers of the Domesday Books included a list of tenants-in-chief as the first item in each county. These institutions and individuals were presumably those primarily liable to tax if it had been levied. The total assessed values for each are not included in Domesday and it is not clear why. The assessed amounts for the individual landholders and tenants in two counties have been counted and are listed in Tables 28 and 29 in the same order as they appear in the Domesday survey.

The amounts are the author's own count. They do not accord precisely with totals recorded by Darby, who totals Cambridgeshire at £1847 and Huntingdon at £827 (1977, 359).

The order in which they are listed in these parts of Domesday is:

i) King,
ii) Religious holdings,
iii) laymen.

Within those categories they are listed in a hierarchical order of precedence. The entries are clearly not listed by order of the size of holding in the counties for any of the categories. For instance, Count Alan has the largest assessment in Cambridgeshire, but is not the first listed of the lay persons.

In Cambridgeshire, the five largest (out of 44) landholders have 61% of the assessed value. Note that the Abbot of Ely and Count Alan each hold about 17% of the total assessed value. Picot of Cambridge has a large holding but is well down the list.

In Huntingdonshire there are 29 landholders. The King and three others hold 63% of the assessed value. Note particularly that Ramsey Abbey holds 21% of the total assessed value.

TABLE 28. Landholders in Cambridgeshire

Cambridgeshire	£	s	d
King	276	6	4
Bishop of Winchester	33	–	–
Bishop of Lincoln	19	–	–
Bishop of Rochester	2	–	–
Abbot of Ely	323	17	–
Abbot of St Edmunds		7	–
Abbot of Ramsey	62	7	0
Abbot of Thorney	6	–	–
Abbot of Crowland	15	10	0
Abbot of St Wandrilles	12	–	–
Abbot of Chatteris	12	2	4
Count Mortain	10	0	5
Earl Roger	33	17	4
Count Alan	308	5	
Count Eustace	26	8	8
The Canons of Bayeaux	13	–	–
Walter Giffard	40	2	–
William of Warenne	51	5	–
Richard s of Count Giffard	1	10	–
Robert of Tosny	7	10	–
Robert Gernon	32	14	8
Geoffrey of Mandeville	42	18	–
Gilbert of Ghent	3	12	–
Gilbert s of Thorold	8	–	–
Eudo the Steward	26	4	2
Hardwin of scales	87	6	3
Hugh of Bernieres		13	–
Hugh of Port	16	–	–
Aubrey de Vere	78	2	8
Eustace of Huntingdon	5	5	–
Guy of Raimbeaucourt	32	17	–
Picot of Cambridge	139	9	0
Peter of Valognes	1	10	0
Ranulf bro of Ilgar	0	10	0
John s of Waleran	15	–	0
William s of Ansculf		2	–
William of Keynes	8	10	–
Robert Fafiton	14	14	4
David of Argenton	10	0	0
Two of King's carpenters	5	10	0
Countess Judith	52	12	17
Azelina wife of Ralph Tallboys	2	0	0
The wife of Boselin of Dives	1	10	0
Erchenger the baker	3	10	0
TOTAL rounded	£1843		

TABLE 29. Landholders in Huntingdonshire

Huntingdonshire	£	s	d
King	191	–	–
Bishop of Lincoln	58	15	–
Bishop of Coutances		5	–
Ely Abbey	40	–	–
Crowland Abbey	6	–	–
Ramsey Abbey	173	8	–
Thorney Abbey	38	10	–
Peterborough Abbey	13	–	–
Count Eustace	14	10	–
Count of Eu	10	0	0
Earl Hugh	9	0	0
Walter Giffard	4	–	–
William of Warenne	20	14	–
Hugh of Bolbec	5	–	–
Eudo s of Hubert	12	–	–
Swein of Essex	6	–	–
Roger of Ivry	10	–	–
Arnulf of Hesdin	10	–	–
Eustace the sheriff	51	5	–
Countess Judith	93	2	–
Gilbert of Ghent	16	–	–
Aubrey de Vere	16	–	–
William s of Ansculf	2	10	–
Ranulf bro of Ilger	7	–	–
Robert of Fafiton	1	–	–
William the artificer	4	–	–
Ralph s of Osmund	0	0	0
Rohais wife of Richard	4	–	–
The King's thanes	6	11	4
TOTAL rounded	£824		

APPENDIX E

Cornish comparison

The purpose of this appendix is to make a restricted comparison of a pastoral western county. It is drawn from some Domesday statistics using mainly the King's holdings in Cornwall. There are 19 entries (out of 80 in all Cornwall), and most of the royal vills are in the far west. The basic figures are those set out in Table 30.

TABLE 30. Cornwall, selected statistics

Item	King's holdings	King's holdings in acres	County
Area in square miles for county			1348 miles^2
Area in acres for king		180,000	
Hides	100		155
Potential plough-lands	582	70,000	
Actual ploughs	300	36,000	
Ploughs in demesne	48		
Persons	1028		5438
Livestock in GLUs	884		2300
Woodland in square leagues	18	26,000	
Meadow acres	118	118	
Pasture in square leagues	60	85,000	
Value	£119		£662

The main assumption made in the calculations in Table 30 are these. Plough-lands are assumed to be about 120 acres. The area of pasture and woodland are mainly recorded in leagues. For instance, in Connerton (Morris 1979, 1:14) the pasture is recorded as 2 leagues by 1 league. If a league is a mile and a half, or 12 furlongs, as is generally assumed, there are then in the King's holdings pasture of 60 square leagues and woodland of 18 square leagues which with the meadow amounts to more than 110,000 acres as shown in Table 30. The areas calculated can be only approximations because those parts recorded in leagues would mostly have been irregular in shape, with the surveyors using rounded figures for the dimensions. Nevertheless, the figures give some rough indication of the relative sizes of the different categories.

The potential ploughlands are less than 70,000 acres and, thus, less than 40% of the total area. The actual ploughlands are only 20% of the total area (both figures suppose that a ploughland was about 120 acres). This is not unexpected as much of Cornwall, then as now, must have been grazing land rather than arable. However, Domesday does not tell us whether the vill had exclusive grazing on the recorded pasture area or whether it included access to common grazing. It is difficult to explain exactly what the Domesday surveyors were recording and how they were using this data to assess the values.

In upland and pastoral regions agricultural land can be divided into three broad categories. First, there is land that is potentially arable. Second, there is land that cannot be ploughed but can be mowed for hay. Third, there is land that can neither be ploughed nor mowed but is usable for grazing and is often summer grazing only. We might guess that, in Cornwall, the plough-teams indicate the land that was actually used as arable at the date of the survey and that the potential plough-team areas are what the surveyors thought could be converted and used as arable. The meadow is self-explanatory, although the area is surprisingly small. The pasture is the land falling into the third category above. The stock-carrying capacity may, in many mountain and moorland regions, be limited by the productive capacity of the first two of the above categories, which provide the winter keep. However, this is a hilly but not a mountainous area, although the highest point on Bodmin Moor is 420 m above sea level. As is the case now with the native ponies of the region, the stock would probably mostly have not been brought down to lower elevations and have been left out on the moor in the winter and rarely given supplementary feed.

Livestock is recorded in the *Liber Exoniensis*, but not in Domesday. We might suppose that recorded animals greatly under-estimates the actual stock. Using the same calculations as in Appendix C, there are recorded in the King's holding fewer than 900 GLUs. If the area for grazing and haymaking, which consists of one-third of the arable when in fallow and the woodland grazing and the meadow and the pasture, it would amount to about 130,000 acres. A large proportion of the pasture would be rough upland, not very productive and mainly summer grazing. It also might have allowed common access to other vills. Taking these factors into account and supposing that, in Cornwall, 20 acres were at that time required to support one GLU, the area of the King's land might have been capable of supporting more than 6000 GLUs rather than the 900 actually recorded.

The livestock figures for the whole county are similar to the Royal holdings with a total livestock number at about 2300 GLUs, excluding oxen, of which 13,000 in number/1430 GLUs are sheep in a county of about 870,000 acres. Compare this with more arable Essex, with an area of 969,000 acres and recorded GLUs of 12,600, again excluding oxen. It may well be that the full capacity of the land was not then being utilised. That count suggests that Essex was carrying five times the level of livestock than was Cornwall. But then, as now, livestock rearing was probably an important part of the West Country economy and the recorded low livestock figures look questionable, especially as several of the King's vills and about 60 other vills in the county record no stock. This seems improbable. Recording livestock might have been difficult. Was it always possible for the Domesday surveyors to know how many wild mares with foals there were up on the Cornish moor? It seems more likely that the livestock was significantly under-counted. It may be that the livestock figures derived from the *Liber Exoniensis* are consistently under-recorded.

This is only a restricted analysis of a pastoral county, but it probably shows that it was more difficult to arrive at comparable assessments that accurately reflected the land occupier's ability to pay in pastoral counties. The usual Domesday assessment formulae were probably devised for the landscapes of the south-east and served the pastoral counties less well.

APPENDIX F

Capital sales evidence

The purpose of this appendix is to better understand the property market for agricultural sales from the point of view of one major player in the county. There is evidence of capital sales of agricultural land extracted from the *Liber Eliensis* Book as shown in Table 31. The monks of Ely were acquisitive and active in the market. The purpose of recording these transactions in *Liber Eliensis* (Fairweather 2005) was clearly to reinforce their title to these lands. Several of the transactions were executed verbally before witnesses who are often named as a further safeguard to title. There are other records of acquisitions not listed in Table 31. Some are gifts to the monastery. Others are exchanges of land. In others, the area of land is not clearly stated and cannot be analysed. The location in the text of each transaction is shown in Column 1 of Table 31. Note that the figures in columns 5 and 8 are, anachronistically, expressed in £s in decimals for the ease of calculation and comparison.

In the 18 transactions in Table 31, two include buildings which clearly enhance the value. Two have fisheries which might have had some value. Two (Streatham and Stoke) are inexplicable low. Perhaps there was an element of gift to the church with some of the transactions. We do not know the dates of these transactions and whether prices remained constant. This makes any analysis much less informative. For instance, it would be surprising if prices were not depressed after poor harvests and higher after good ones and therefore varied over time. Nevertheless, the remaining transactions, few though they are, show a general pattern. Hides of bare land were worth about £5 per hide to the monks, especially if the land was located not far from Ely.

Other entries in Book II of *Liber Eliensis* indicate that live and dead stock were of appreciable value, although there is not enough information to analyse the recorded figures. Buildings clearly had a value. It would be surprising if this were not so. Transaction 11A in Chippenham (about 20 miles/32 km from Ely) is interesting because it implies they were able to measure land with some precision if need be.

If Domesday is indicating a rental value of about £1 per annum per hide, and this is very likely the case, the ratio of rent to capital value is unexpected. It appears to be about 5 years-purchase, which represents a 20% return. A 10% return (a years-purchase of ten) would be less surprising and thus result in a higher capital value. Perhaps the low capital value in relation to the rental value is an indication of:

i) a thin market,
ii) the risks inherent in medieval agriculture, and
iii) the security of tenure being entirely at the whim of the King.

TABLE 31 (opposite). Sales transactions in *Liber Eliensis* (Fairweather 2005)

Appendix F. Capital sales evidence 141

Liber Eliensis ref in Book II	Vill(s)	Area hides	Acres	Hides/ decimal	Consideration as stated	In £s decimal	Price £ per hide decimal	Comments
1	2	3	4	5	6	7	8	9
10	Streatham	8		8	£60	60	7.5	Bought in two equal parts from two sisters
10	Streatham	2			20 Mancuses	2.5	1.25	Including two weirs
11	Downham	2		2	£15	15	7.5	The *Liber* notes that it is 'a vill which is very fertile'
11	Downham (Clayhithe)	5		5	£15	15	3	Other conditions concern a silver cup worth 40s. It also includes livestock and dead stock
11	Downham	1		1	£4 as part of equality of exchange	4	4	This was an exchange of 2 hides for 3 hides with the consideration paid for the equality of exchange
11	Downham	2		2	100s	5	2.5	Paid separately for all the 'corn which was on the land' with all the stock
11A	Chippenham	3		3.00	100s per hide	15	5.0	It was later found that there were only 226 acres and there was not good title to 82 of those acres
12	Witchford		200	1.67	£11	11	6.6	
16	Haddenham		26	0.22	£7	7	32.3	A farm with buildings on it. It might be supposed that the greater part of the value related to the buildings
17	Wilburton	2		2.00	90 mancuses	11.25	5.6	Includes five farm buildings
21	Doddington and Wimblington		60	0.50	100s	5	10.0	Includes a weir yielding 1000 eels
22	Wimblington		10	0.08	20s	1	12.0	Includes 2 fisheries
31	Fordham and Milton	2	37	2.31	£11	11	4.8	
31	Holland in Essex	5		5.00	£20	20	4.0	
39	Stoke near Ipswich	10		10.00	100 mancuses	12.5	1.3	Includes 2 mills (but no indication why it was so cheap)
44	Weeting	3		3.00	6	6	2.0	
45	Horningsea	2		2.00	£8	8	4.0	
49a	Houghton Beds	2		2.00	£4	4	2.0	

APPENDIX G

Cambridgeshire Shire Reeve Picot's property empire

The purpose of this appendix is to examine and partly quantify the role of the Shire Reeve of Cambridgeshire in 1086. We can identify, mainly from Domesday, six streams of revenue as listed in columns numbered 1–6 in Table 32, all available to Picot either directly *ex-officio* or from lands acquired indirectly linked to his power and status as Shire Reeve.

In all six cases the gross revenue available to Picot is over-stated because it supposes that successful collection rates were near 100%. This is never the case. On the other hand the revenues in rows 1 and 2 may be under-stated because Picot would also have had the income from soke and sake in his manors.

The revenue from the Shire Reeve's duties in relation to the Royal estates in row 8 is difficult to estimate and depends on the functions required. The

TABLE 32. Picot's sources of revenue

	Revenue stream	Gross	Multiplier	Gross revenue to Picot	Comments
1	Rental value from 44 tenancies as listed in the survey	£139	1	£139	Assuming that Picot received at least as much rental income as the recorded 1086 values
2	Profit from 20 sub-tenancies as listed in the survey, at say £3 each	£60	1	£60	Assuming each sub-tenancy made a profit of about the same amount as the rental value
3	Income from mill(s) in Cambridge	£5	1	£5	Apportioned from the total value in of £9 for Cambridge mills. Picot has 3 'mills' listed, but more probably it is 3 millstones in 1 mill
4	Duties in relation to heriots as listed in Cambridge DB entry	£8	1	£8	Also additional benefits such as a riding horse as listed in Domesday but no value added her
5	Managing Royal holdings which in Cambridgeshire had a total 1086 rental value of £276. The value of Royal lands from DB	£276	0.1	£28	Management fees for rental properties are seldom below 10%
6	Exemption for his lands from a (say) 4s geld for the service of collecting the tax	£139	0.2	£28	Picot would only benefit in the years when a geld was levied. This figure supposes that the exemption did not apply to the sub-tenancies
	TOTAL			£268	Gross revenue

management of landed estates is expensive. If all the entire management and collection duties were devolved by the Crown to the Shire Reeves the cost figure of 10% of the revenue (that is 0.1 as used in this analysis) is too low. The present Royal Estates, that is the Crown Estates and the Duchy of Cornwall, often have cost to yield ratios of more than 20%. However, it might have been the case that not all the management functions were devolved to Shire Reeves.

The total revenue of approximately £268 does not represent a net income available to Picot. It represents the approximate size of the funds passing through his hands. There were, in all the six cases, costs to be incurred by Picot in relation to management, collection and other duties required to obtain the revenue streams. The cost to yield would have differed for each revenue stream. As almost £200 was revenue from his own lands, the net income could have been in total about 50% of the gross revenue. Picot was rich, although little of his empire was heritable.

The figures cannot be exact and they do no more than indicate the approximate size and scope of Picot's extensive property empire within Cambridgeshire. Other Shire Reeves would have had access to similar streams of revenue.

APPENDIX H

Surveying a village

The purpose of this appendix is to illustrate the process of understanding and sorting the information on the ground and then selecting and expressing the relevant data in the format of the survey. This is illustrated by a fictional village with circumstances that are uncomplicated and not unusual in the eastern counties.

The vill is of medium size: about 2100 acres. About 20% of the land is taken up by the sites of houses with their gardens, sites of other buildings, a church and churchyard, roads and tracks and other unused lands. The size of the vill in acres would not be accurately known to the inhabitants or the visiting surveyors.

Before inspection, the Domesday surveyors would know that the vill answers for five hides and is occupied by a single manor which they believe to be held by Hugo of Poissy, and that no part is sub-let. They would expect the vill to be average in size, productive and typical of the county.

The surveyors would ascertain the following information through i) existing information derived from the Hidage assessments and the existing administration records, ii) physical inspection while in the vill, and iii) evidence given on oath, using the existing procedures of the manor courts, from nine named persons of the Hundred with local knowledge and from some others.

- Those giving evidence confirm that the manor is held by Hugo and no part of it is sub-let;
- They would be told that all the lands of the manor lie within the vill and there are no outliers;
- No one giving evidence raised any issue relating to Hugo's entitlement to the manor, although those giving evidence named the English holder of the land prior to Hugo;
- They are informed that there are now seven ploughlands with a sufficient number of ploughs and oxen present in the manor;
- They see that the ploughlands are arranged in three fields divided into furlong strips;
- Two of the ploughlands are in-hand;
- The other ploughlands are with the peasants;
- There are five villagers and ten smallholders attached by custom to the lands of the vill;
- There is woodland for 70 pigs;
- There are 100 acres of meadow;

- There are 450 acres of pasture;
- They are informed that there are 15 cows, 12 pigs and 200 sheep;
- Those giving evidence consider the values were much the same TRE and when acquired.

In addition they might note that the full workforce in the vill, including women and youths and those working part time in agriculture, farming the land and managing the woodland and working in various capacities for the demesne and its land is more than 120 persons. There are ten others living in the village not directly occupied with agricultural work, including a rector and curate. They can see that there are about 15 timber and thatch houses and other buildings, of which three are substantial construction and others of varying quality. There is a church and churchyard. They might enquire from the Rector about the level of tithes. These items are not of direct concern to the assessment but give an indication of the prosperity of the vill. They do not survey or count the houses and buildings. They do not measure or count the mature timber trees. They do not take a census of the population.

The Domesday surveyors must make judgements on behalf of the commissioners about several matters and their opinions are as follows.

- The number of ploughlands is correctly assessed at seven;
- There is not at present any scope to expand the arable;
- The soil is a productive medium light, loam and typical of the Hundred;
- They consider there is sufficient meadow and grazing on the pastures and in woodland to maintain the livestock and ox teams;
- They estimate that the underwood areas of the woodland are sufficient for the needs of the vill;
- They see no particular disadvantages and consider it should be valued at the same level per ploughland as others in the Hundred and county; and
- They value the land at £1 per ploughland.

The entry in Great Domesday after editing, in the list of Hugo's holdings in that county under the relevant Hundred, will therefore be as follows in the English translation.

> In {*name of vill*} Hugo holds 5 hides. Land for 7 ploughs. in lordship 2 ploughs. 5 villagers and 10 small holders have 5 ploughs, meadow for 7 ploughs; woodland for 70 pigs; pasture for the livestock, value now and always £7.

The list in abbreviated Latin, but without the abbreviation marks, might be as follows.

> In {*vill*} ten Hugo V hid. Tra.e.VII. car. In dnio.II.car.
> Ibi.V.uitti cu.X.hnt.V.car.
> Ptu.VII.car. Silva.LXX.porc. Pasta ad pecun villae. Val et valuit. VII. Lib.

Bibliography

Ash, H.B. (1947) *Columella, On Agriculture*. Cambridge MA: Harvard University Press.

Bates, D. (2018) *William the Conqueror*. New Haven CO: Yale University Press.

Bede. *Ecclesiastical History of the English People* (eds D. Farmer and L. Sherley-Price, 1990). London Penguin Classics.

Bowden, P.J. (ed.) (1990) *Economic Change: wages, profits and rents 1550–1750*. Cambridge: Cambridge University Press.

Choquer, G. and Favory, G.F. (2001) *L'arpentage romain*. Paris: Editions Errance.

Clancy, M.T. (2003) *From Memory to Written Record England 1066–1307*. Oxford: Blackwell.

Cleargot, P. (2003) *The Origins of the French General Cadastre*. Unpublished working paper, Federation Internationale des Geometres (FIG) conference April 2003. https://www.fig.net/resources/proceedings/fig_proceedings/fig_2003/PS_1/PS1_2_Clergeot.pdf

Dalby, A. (2010) *Cato on Farming, De Agricultura*. London: Prospect Books.

Darby, H.C. (1977) *Domesday England*. Cambridge: Cambridge University Press.

Delaine, J. (1997) *The Baths of Caracalla*. Plymouth RI: *Journal of Roman Archaeology* Supplementary Series 25.

Dowell, S. (1965) [1884] *A History of Taxation and Taxes in England*. London: Routledge.

Duncan-Jones, R. (1994) *Money and Government in the Roman Empire*. Cambridge: Cambridge University Press.

Dyer, C. (2009) *Making a Living in the Middle Ages*. New Haven CO: Yale University Press.

Erskine, R.W.H. and Williams, R.A. (eds) (2003) *The Story of Domesday Book*. Chichester: Phillimore.

Fairweather, J. (2005) *Liber Eliensis*. Wadebridge: Boydell Press.

Fitzherbert, J. (1882) [1534] *The Boke of husbandry*. London: Trubner & Co.

Fitzpatrick, P. (1941) *Jock of the Bushveld*. London: Longman Green & Co.

Galbraith, V.H. (1974) *Domesday. Its place in Administrative History*. Oxford: Clarendon.

George, H. (1881) *Progress and Poverty*. New York: D. Appleton and Co.

Grierson, P. (2003) The monetary system under William I. In Erskine and Willaims (eds), 112–18.

Grigg, D. (2019) *Farm Size in England and Wales from Early Victorian Times to the Present*. Acccessed online through University of California Press. Accessed on line 2019. Available at https://www.bahs.org.uk/AGHR/ARTICLES/35n2a6.pdf

Gullick, M. (2003) The Great and Little Domesday manuscripts. In Erskine and Williams (eds) *The story of the Domesday Book*, 93–112.

Haigh, M. (2015) *Open Field Farming in Laxton*. Laxton: Laxton Local History Group.

Hamilton, N. (1876) *Inquisito Comitatus Cantabridgeinsis & Inquisito Eliensis*. London: Royal Society of literature.

Hart, C. (1974) *The Hidation of Cambridgeshire*. Leicester: Leicester University Press.

Harvey, S. (2014) *Domesday, Book of Judgement*. Oxford: Oxford University Press.

Henderson, E. (1896) *Select Documents of the Middle Ages*. London: George Bell and Sons.

HM Land Registry (2017) *Report and Accounts*. www.gov.uk.

Ingram, J. and Giles, J.J.A. (1847) *Anglo-Saxon Chronicle*. Pantianos Classics eBook edition.

Keith, S. (1993) *Property Tax in Anglophone Africa: a practical manual*. Washington DC: World Bank.

Keith, S. (2017) A study of Domesday watermills in the Cambridgeshire landscape. *Proceedings of the Cambridge Antiquarian Society* 106, 49–60.

Keith, S. (2018) *Why are so Few Domesday mills recorded in Cornwall and Devon?* Mills Archive website. Simon Keith, 16 Jan 2018 [https://new.millsarchive.org/2018/01/16/why-are-so-few-domesday-mills-recorded-in-cornwall-and-devon-a-new-thesis/5/].

Lamont, E. and Cunningham, E.W. (1890) *Walter of Henley's Husbandry*. London: Longman Green and Co.

Langdon, J. (1986) *Horses Oxen and Technical Innovation*. Cambridge: Cambridge University Press.

Lennard, R. (1960) The composition of demesne plough-teams in twelfth-century England. *English Historical Review* 75, 193–205.

Loyn, H.R. (1962) *Anglo-Saxon England and the Norman Conquest.* London: Longman.

Maitland, F.W. (1989) [1897] *Domesday and Beyond.* Cambridge: Cambridge University Press.

Maslow, A.H. (1943) A theory of human motivation. *Psychological Review* 50(4), 370–96.

McDonald, J. and Snook, J.G.D. (1985) Were the tax assessments of Domesday England artificial? The case for Essex. *Economic History Review* 38(3), 353–73.

McDonald, J. and Snook, J.G.D. (1986) *Domesday Economy: a new approach to Anglo-Norman history.* Oxford: Clarendon.

McErlean, T. and Crothers, T.N. (2007) *Harnessing the Tides.* Dublin: Stationery Office.

Minchinton, W.E. (1977) *Tidemills of England and Wales. Transactions of the Fourth symposium of The International Molinological Society*, 339–53. London: Wind and Watermills Section, Society for the Protection of Ancient Buildings.

Morris, J. (1975) *Domesday Book 19 Huntingdonshire.* Chichester: Phillimore.

Morris, J. (1976) *Domesday Book 12 Hertfordshire.* Chichester: Phillimore.

Morris, J. (1977) *Domesday Book 28 Nottinghamshire.* Chichester: Phillimore.

Morris, J. (1979) *Domesday Book 10 Cornwall.* Chichester: Phillimore.

Morris, J. (1981) *Domesday Book 18 Cambridgeshire.* Chichester: Phillimore.

Morris, J. (1983) *Domesday Book 32 Essex.* Chichester: Phillimore.

Morris, J. (1985) *Domesday Book 33 Norfolk.* Philimore Chichester.

Morris, J. (1986) *Domesday book 31 Lincolnshire.* Chichester: Phillimore.

Nix 2019 appx 1

Office of National Statistics (2018) *200 years of the Census in Cambridgeshire.* www.statistics.gov.uk.

Office of National Statistics (2020) *The UK national balance sheet Table 7.* www.ons.gov.uk.

Oosthuizen, S. (2013) *The Anglo-Saxon Fenland.* Oxford: Windgather Press.

Otway-Ruthven, J. (1938) ICC 400. In Sulzman 1938, 427.

Pollock, F. and Maitland, F.F.W. (1959) [1895] *History of English Law.* Washington DC: Lawyers Literary Club.

Postan, M. (1993) *The Medieval Economy and Society.* London: Penguin.

Rackham, O. (1986) *The History of the Countryside.* London: J.M. Dent and Sons.

Ravenscroft, N. (2001) *Good practice guidelines for agricultural leasing arrangements.* Rome: FAO. [http://www.fao.org/agroecology/database/detail/ru/c/1202190/]

Redmond, G. (2018) *The John Nix Farm Management Pocketbook for 2019* (49th edn). Melton Mowbray: Agro Business Consultants.

Ricardo, D. (1971) [1817] *The Principles of Political Economy and Taxation.* London: Penguin.

Richardson, H.G. (1942) The medieval plough-team. *History* 26, 287–96.

Roffe, D. (2000) *The Inquest and the Book.* Oxford: Oxford University Press.

Round, J.H. (1909) *Feudal England.* London: George Allen & Unwin.

Royal Institute of Chartered Surveyors (RIC) (2014) *RICS Valuation – Professional Standards.* London: Royal Institute of Chartered Surveyors.

Seebohm, F. (1905) *The English Village Community.* London: Longmans.

Sulzman, L.F. (1938) *Inquisitio Comitatus Cantabrigiensis.* London: Victoria County History of Cambridgeshire volume 1.

Tolstoy, L. (2004) [1878] *Anna Karenina.* New York: Dover Publishers.

Vitruvius. *The Ten Books on Architecture* (Trans. M.H. Morgan 1914). New York: Dover publications.

Watson, J.A. and More, J.A.S. (1956) *Agriculture The Science and Practice of British Farming* (10th edn). London: Oliver and Boyd.

Welldon Finn, R. (1960) The Inquisition Eliensis reconsidered. *English Historical Review* 75 385–409.

Welldon Finn, R. (1961) *The Domesday Inquest.* London: Longmans.

Welldon Finn, R. (1964) *Liber Exoniensis.* London: Longmans.

Whittaker, T.P. (1914) *The Ownership, Tenure and Taxation of Land.* London: Macmillan.

Willams, A. and Martin, A.G.H. (2003) *Domesday Book, a complete translation.* London: Penguin.

Young, A. (1768) *A Six Weeks Tour Through the Southern Counties of England and Wales.* London: W. Nicoll.

Index

Page numbers in **bold** indicate tables, and those in *italic* indicate figures. Page numbers followed by 'n' indicate footnotes.

Abington Pigots, vill (Cambs.) 28, 92, *94*
ad firmam, meaning 61–2
ad valorem property lists 21, 22, 33, 39–40, 44 (Box 4), 68, 105, 107
    property tax options 29–31, **30**
Africa
    land tenure and taxation 7, **30**, 40
    use of oxen 130
agricultural labour
    and definition of hide 52–3
    labour duties on in-hand land 116
    numbers recorded in Domesday in relation to agricultural labour requirements 69, 110, 121–6
agriculture
    agrarian land use in 1086 69, 127–34
    agricultural and estate management, 11th century 115–20
    agricultural land tenure, forms of 6–8
    agricultural potential, influence on rental values 65, 69–71
    arable crop yields 49, 59–60, 118
    Cornwall, comparative study 11, 137–9, *137*
    Domesday focus on agrarian economy 48–9, 110–11
    farmland in boroughs 80, **80**
    recording of agricultural assets 42, 48–9
    sequence for arable cultivation 117–18
    size of agricultural holdings 52–3
    see also agricultural labour; dairy farming; farm buildings; livestock
aides and subsidies 3, 9, 30, 70 (Box 6), 109
Alan, Count 8–9, **28**, 135, **136**
Anglesey, hides recorded by Bede 49, **50**, *51*
Anglo-Saxon Chronicle 3, 60, 72, 111, 131
    on meeting at Christmas 1085 99
annual sums, as basis for assessment 29, 55–9
    see also rents
arable land *see* agriculture
Armingford Hundred (Cambs.)
    agrarian land use in 1086 127–34, **127**, *133*

agricultural labour, numbers recorded 121–6, **121**, **122**
geographic order in ICC 92–3
land farmed in-hand 115
and logistics of Domesday *94*, 96, **96**, **99**, 100, *100*
ploughlands 29, 31n6, 62–3, *63*
reduced hides 36, **37**
Royal holdings 71
study area 11, **11**
survey entries 97
TRE values 73
assessments 'when acquired' 74, 76
assessors, and logistics of Domesday 89, 92
Australia 17, 70 (Box 6)

bailiffs 89, 115, 116, 125
Bassetlaw Wapentake (Notts.) 21n9, 63, 73n13, 92n4
Bassingbourn, vill (Cambs.) 27–8, **28**, 92, *94*
Bath (Som.) **66**, *67*
Battersea (Surrey), mills 66n9
Bede, and concept of the hide 49–50, **50**, *51*
Bedford **66**, *67*, 79, 83
Bedfordshire, TRE assessments 73, 74
Bodmin (Cornwall) **66**, *67*
boroughs 79–84, 113
    proximity to urban centres, influence on agricultural rental values 65, 66, **66**
Brecklands 68, 75
buildings
    in boroughs 79–82, **80**, 83–4
    outside boroughs, omitted from Domesday 39–42, 43–4, 110
    see also farm buildings
burghal Hidages 83, 84
Business Rates 30, **30**

cadastral taxes 58
    see also Napoleonic cadastral tax
cadastres 15, 106
Cambridge 80–2, **80**, *81*
    mills 83, 91, **142**
    population 79n1, 125n10
    proximity to, influence on agricultural rental values 66, **66**, *67*

Index

Cambridgeshire
   geographical ownership patterns 27–8, **28**
   landholders, assessed values 135, **136**
   records of irregularity or disputed title 18
   study areas 10–11, **11**
   TRE assessments 73–4, **73**
   see also Armingford Hundred; *individual places by name*
capital sales evidence 55, 140, **141**
capital values, as basis for assessment 55
car (*caruca*) 3, 33
carucate, relation to hide 53–4
Cato, *De agricultura* 115, 117n4, 119, 123n7, 129n2
cattle 127–8, **128**, 133–4
   see also oxen
Centuria, Roman, and hide 50
Cheveley Hundred (Cambs.) 37, 92
Chillingham Park (Northumb.) 128 (Box 7)
Chippenham, vill (Cambs.) 70 (Box 6), 140, **141**
Christmas 1085 meeting at Gloucester 86, 98, 99, 103, 111, 112
churches 33, 35, 41
Clavering half Hundred (Essex) 11, **11**
   actual or potential ploughlands **63**
   agrarian land use in 1086 127–34, **127**, **133**
   agricultural labour, numbers recorded 121–6, **121**, **122**
   reduced hides 36
   Royal holdings 71, 73–4
   woodland grazing 46
Clopton, vill (Cambs.) 92, *94*
Colchester (Essex) 79–82, **80**, *81*, 83
Columella, *On Agriculture* 115, 123n7
common rights 7, 27, 138
Community Charge (poll tax) (1990) 109, 112
consistency, Domesday achievement 10
coppicing 45, 46, 47–8, 123
Cornwall
   comparative study 11, 137–9, **137**
   hides and ploughlands 36, 63, 137–8, **137**
   livestock 49, 69, 111, **137**, 138–9
   TRE assessments 73
   value and distance from London 66
   woodland 47, 137, **137**, 138
Council Tax 30, 108n3
County Reeves *see* Shire Reeves
crop rotation, 2-field and 3-field systems 53, 118, 129, 132, **133**
Crown *see* Royal holdings; William I, King
Croydon, vill (Cambs.) 92, *94*
Croydon Wilds (Cambs.) 68n10

dairy farming 49, 122n2, 130
Danegeld 9, 20, 31, **107**, 108
   see also Hidage assessment system
deeds registers 16, 17
demesne land *see* in-hand
demesnes, hierarchy of 8–9, **8**
derelict buildings *see* buildings
'Dialogue Concerning the Exchequer, The' 31
Doddington (Cambs.) **141**
Domesday Book
   achievement 105–6, 114
   content and omissions 25–54, 110–11, 112–13
   fictional village survey 144–5
   as fiscal failure 108–9, 114
   in historic context of taxation 106–10, **107**
   logistics 85–104, 111–12, 113, 144–5
   purpose 14–24, 113
   surveyor's perspective 1–13
   valuation 55–78, 111, 113
   see also boroughs; consistency; geography; manpower; preparatory stages; sequence of events; terms of reference; timescale
Dorchester (Dorset) 66, *67*
Dorset 11
Downham, vill (Cambs.) **141**
dwellings *see* buildings

East Hatley, vill, (Cambs.) 92, *94*
East India Company 19 (Box 2), 24
editing and production of written list, logistics 101–2
Ely Abbey xiii (Box 1)
   holdings in Cambridgeshire and Huntingdonshire, assessed values 135, **136**
   sales transactions 140, **141**
   see also Liber Eliensis
Essex
   actual or potential ploughlands 63–4, **63**
   livestock 138
   see also Clavering half Hundred; Little Domesday; *individual places by name*
estate management 115–20
   estate terriers 16, 19–21, 117
   as reason for compiling property lists 16
Eudo the Steward xiii (Box 1), **136**
exemptions from tax 30–1
Exeter (Devon) 66, *67*
Exeter Book *see Liber Exoniensis*

farm buildings 35, 41, 117, 140, **141**
farm labourers *see* agricultural labour
Fens, soil and land quality 68
feudal system 8–9, 22–3, 94, 116, 126
   see also tenants-in-chief
field surveys, logistics 99–100

Finance Act (1909/10) *see* Increment Value Duty
fisheries 34, 35, 42, 140, **141**
Fordham (Cambs.) **141**
France, taxation
    Napoleonic cadastral tax 9, 19 (Box 2), 23, 57, 58 (Box 5), 112
    quota taxes of the *Ancien Regime* 9, 30n5, 58 (Box 5), 61n4, 112

Gamlingay (Cambs.) xiii (Box 1), 96
gelds 38 (Box 3), 44 (Box 4), 54, 98
    paid by boroughs 82, 83, 84
    see also Danegeld; Hidage assessment system
geography
    counties and circuits 5
    geographic focus of study 10–11
    geographic order of ICC 92–3
    geographical ownership patterns 27–9
George, Henry (1839–97) 44 (Box 4), 106n2
Gloucester, meeting at Christmas 1085 **86**, 98, 99, 103, 111, 112
GLU (Grazing Livestock Units) 124n9, 127–8, **128**, 131, **133**, 138
goats 127, **128**
grain, crop yields 49, 59–60, 118
grazing
    Cornwall 138
    Grazing Livestock Units (GLU) 124n9, 127–8, **128**, 131, **133**, 138
    pasture **34**, 42, 69, 110, 134
    woodland pasture 32–3, **34**, 45, 46–7, 69, 110, 123, **128**, **133**, 134
gross annual output, as basis for assessment 55–7
Grosseteste, Robert, bishop of Lincoln 110, 115–20
Guilden Morden, vill (Cambs.) 28, 92, *94*

Haddenham, vill (Cambs.) **141**
Hardwin of Scales 8, 26, **28**
harvest, labour requirements 53, 123
Hatley, vill *see* East Hatley
Hatley St George (Cambs.) 46
Hatley Wilds (Cambs.) 68n10
haywards 116
hearth taxes 9, 70 (Box 6)
Henley, Walter of, *Husbandry* 110, 115–20, 123n6
hereditaments 25
Herefordshire 11, 73
Hereward 26, 76
Hertfordshire 73
    see also Odsey Hundred
Hidage assessment system 9, 10, 30–1, 38 (Box 3), 76, 77
    as basis for Domesday 15, 20, 21, 23, 24, 105, 112, 113
    and ICC 93, 95

    and logistics of Domesday 85, 87, 96, 98, 99
    superior to Domesday as taxation base 108, 109
    see also Burghal Hidages; Danegeld; hides
hides
    assessment in hides, in typical Domesday entry **34**
    concept of 49–54, **50**, *51*
    relationship to ploughlands in Domesday 36–9, **37**, 54, 63, **63**, 105, 114
hierarchy of demesnes 8–9, **8**
Holland, vill (Essex) **141**
Horningsea, vill (Cambs.) **141**
horses 118, 127, **128**, 130n3, 130n5, 131–2, 134
Houghton, vill (Beds.) **141**
houses *see* buildings
Hundreds, as unit for tax assessment 9
Huntingdon 66, **66**, *67*, 80, **80**, *81*
Huntingdonshire
    jurors 90
    landholders, assessed values 135, **136**
    records of irregularity or disputed title 18
    study areas 10–11, **11**
    TRE assessments 73, 74
    see also Toseland Hundred; *individual places by name*
'Husbandry', treatise 115–20

ICC *see* Inquisitio Comitatus Cantabrigiensis (ICC)
IE *see* Inquisitio Eliensis (IE)
in-hand, land farmed
    demesne land and net profit system 57–9
    focus of medieval agricultural treatises 115–16, 120
income tax 56–7, 106, 107, 109, 112
Increment Value Duty, national survey under Finance Act 1909/10 12, 23, 40, 40n11, 106–7, **107**
Indian subcontinent
    Land Revenue Taxation 19 (Box 2), 23, 24
    see also Pakistan
Inland Revenue
    Valuation Office 102, 106–7
    see also Increment Value Duty
Inquisitio Comitatus Cantabrigiensis (ICC) 3, 11, **11**
    actual or potential ploughlands 63, **63**
    analysis of data, comparison with Domesday 31–3, **34**
    evidence for agrarian land use 127–34, **127**, **133**
    hierarchy of tenures 8
    and logistics of Domesday 87, 89, 90, 91, 92–3, 94–8, **96**, 102
    as precedent for Domesday 95–8
    relationship with IE 20
Inquisitio Eliensis (IE) 3, 26–7
    analysis of data, comparison with Domesday 31–3, **34**
    as estate terrier 20
    hierarchy of tenures 8
    terms of reference (IE/TOR) 32–3

Inquisitio Gheldi see Liber Exoniensis
Iona, hides recorded by Bede 49, **50**, *51*
irrigation systems, taxation of users 16n3

judicial hearings 100–1, **100**, 144–5
jurors, so-called 89, 90
jury hearings 88–90, 92, 93, 101

King *see* Royal holdings; William I

labourers *see* agricultural labour
land measurement 70 (Box 6), 119
land registration, and Domesday 16–19
Land Registry of England and Wales 17
Land Tax, English 23, 107, **107**, 109, 112
land tenure, forms of agricultural land tenure 6–8
landholders
    hierarchy of demesnes 8–9, **8**
    potential tax implications 135, **136**
    see also tenants-in-chief
legal ownership, recording 16–19
Liber Eliensis 3, 26, 76
    evidence for land measurement 70 (Box 6)
    oral grants 16, 140
    on Picot 91
    sales transactions 140, **141**
Liber Exoniensis (Exeter Book) 3, 31, 94–5, 96, 97–8, 111
    Inquisitio Gheldi 16n4, 21, 30, 82
    on livestock 32, **34**, 69, 97, 111, 131, 138–9
Lincoln 80–2, **80**, *81*
Litlington, vill (Cambs.) 27–8, **28**, 92, *94*
Little Domesday
    areas covered 5
    evidence for agrarian land use 127–34, **127**, **133**
    information recorded 32, **34**, 36, 42, 49
    logistics 87, 94, 95, 97–8, 101–2
    valuations 73–4
    see also Clavering half Hundred
livestock
    Cornwall 49, 69, 111, **137**, 138–9
    Ely Abbey estates 140, **141**
    in ICC and other surveys 32, **34**, 96, 97, 127–34
    labour requirements 123, 125
    and land use 69, 127–34
    limited information in Domesday 32, **34**, 49, 97, 110, 111
    management, evidence from medieval agricultural treatises 119
    see also cattle; goats; horses; oxen; pigs; sheep
London
    distance from, influence on agricultural rental values 66, **66**
    omitted from Domesday 84

Longstowe Hundred (Cambs.) xiii, **37**, 96

Man, Isle of, hides recorded by Bede 49, **50**, *51*
manerium, meaning 40
manor, as unit of assessment 9, 25
manor courts 97, 100, 144
manor houses, omitted from Domesday 40–1
manpower
    required for compiling Domesday 88, 99–100, **99**, 101, 102–3, 112
    see also agricultural labour
markets, access to 45, 49, 65, 66
mass appraisal 12–13
meadow, in typical Domesday entry **34**
measurement *see* land measurement
Melbourn, vill (Cambs.) 28, **28**, 92, *94*
Meldreth, vill (Cambs.) 28, **28**, 92, *94*
military services 4
mills 41, 42, 66n9
    see also watermills
Milton (Cambs.) **141**
monasteries
    buildings 41
    religious holdings in Cambridgeshire and Huntingdonshire, assessed values 135, **136**
    see also Ely Abbey
Monthly Assessments (Commonwealth period) 107, 109, 112

Napoleonic cadastral tax 9, 19 (Box 2), 23, 57, 58 (Box 5), 112
net output or average profit, as basis for assessment 57–9
Netherlands 9n3, 19 (Box 2), 58
Northstow Hundred (Cambs.) **37**, 92
Nottinghamshire 11
    TRE assessments 73
    unit of assessment 25n1
    woodland pasture 32–3, **34**, 47
    see also Bassetlaw Wapentake

octroi 83
Odsey Hundred (Herts.) 28–9, **28**
omissions from Domesday 39–48, 110–11, 112–13
open fields 29, 124n9, 130, 132
oral grants 16, 140
Orwell, vill 28, **28**
oxen *37*, 53–4, 118, 128–31, 133–4, **133**, 138
Oxford **66**, *67*

Pakistan 19 (Box 2), 56, 59n1
Papacy, taxation 9, 43, 70 (Box 6)
Papworth Hundred (Cambs.) **37**, 92
pasture *see* grazing

perch, size of 70 (Box 6), 119
personnel *see* manpower
'Peter's pence' (Papal tax) 9, 43, 70 (Box 6)
physical inspections, logistics 88–93
Picot of Cambridge, Shire Reeve for Cambridgeshire 8, 9, 26, 31, 91–2
   holdings in Cambridgeshire, assessed values 135, **136**
   property empire 142–3, **143**
pigs 119, 127–8, **128**
   woodland grazing 46, 128
plough-teams
   and calculations of land use 131, **133**
   comparison with ICC 96, **96**
   number of oxen 129–30; *see also* ploughing with oxen
   and translation of *car* 3, 33
   see also ploughlands
ploughing with oxen 37, 53–4, 118, 129–30, 131, 133–4, **133**
ploughlands
   actual or potential 34, 62–4, **63**
   as basis for assessment 29, 105, 111
   Cornwall 137–8, **137**
   as formal fiscal measure of arable land for a plough-team 129, 131
   relationship to hides 36–9, **37**, 54, 63, **63**, 105, 113
   and translation of *car* 3, 33
   in typical Domesday entry **34**, 35
poll taxes 9, 109, 112
population size, evidence for 79
   and Domesday figures for agricultural labourers 69, 110, 121–6
possession, land registers recording possession rather than ownership 17–18
preparatory stages before fieldwork, logistics 98
property lists
   Domesday as property list 1–13
   see also ad valorem property lists
property market *see* capital sales evidence
provosts 116

quantum taxes 9–10
   see also tithe
quarrying 42
quota taxes 9–10
   France, *Ancien Regime* 9, 30n5, 58 (Box 5), 61n4, 112
   see also Rating system

rack rents 25, 30, 59, 64, 65
Ramsey Abbey 135, **136**
Rating system 9–10, 15, 17–18n5, 25, 29–30, **30**, 61, 62, 107, **107**
   Valuation Lists 12, 23, 107
redere, use in Domesday 60
reeves 53, 68, 89, 125
   see also Shire Reeves
rent rolls 16, 19
rents and rental values, as basis for assessment 59–60, 64–5, 105–6
   boroughs, rents paid/due listed rather than rental values 82, 83
   determining rental levels 76–7
   factors affecting rental values 65–71
   relation of rental value to capital value, Ely Abbey estates 140
   rental value dispersion 65
   rental value or rent passing 60–1, 111, 113
Ricardo, David 44, 44 (Box 4)
Robert, Bishop of Hereford (d. 1095) 37–9
Roger, Earl 28, **28**, 136
Roman period
   Centuria, and hide 50
   land measurement 70 (Box 6)
   taxation 16n3, 75
   treatises on agriculture 115, 117n4, 123n7; *see also* Cato
root title 18–19n7
Royal holdings
   actual or potential ploughlands 63–4, **63**
   Cambridgeshire and Huntingdonshire, assessed values 135, **136**
   Cornwall, comparative study of pastoral county 11, 137–9, **137**
   hierarchy of demesnes 8–9, **8**
   and purpose of Domesday 20–1, 39
   role of Shire Reeve 142–3
   title changes 26
   valuation 71–2, **71**, 76

Salisbury (Wilts.) **66**, *67*
   meeting at Lammas 1086 99, 101
saltworks 33, 35, 42
Sassines, Register of 17
Scotland 17, 59, 112
scutage 4
self-assessment for taxation 90–1
seneschals 89, 115, 116
'Seneschals', treatise on husbandry 115–20
sequence of events, logistics 94–5
share-cropping arrangements 7, 59n1
sheep 117, 119, 127, 127n1, **128**, 138
Shepreth, vill 28, **28**
sheriff, exemption of lands from tax 31
Shingay, vill (Cambs.) 92, *94*
Shire Reeves (County Reeves) 20, **88**, 91–2, 98, 142–3
   see also Picot of Cambridge
Site Value Rating 44 (Box 4)
soil and land quality, influence on rental values 65, 68
Stamford (Lincs.) 80, **80**, *81*

Staploe Hundred (Cambs.) 36, **37**, 92
Steeple Morden, vill (Cambs.) 28, 92, *94*
Stoke near Ipswich, vill (Suffolk) 140, **141**
Streatham, vill (Cambs.) 140, **141**
Stroma (Orkneys) 128 (Box 7)
sub-tenants, named in typical Domesday entry **34**
subsidies *see* aides and subsidies
Suffolk 11, 41n12
   see also Little Domesday
sulung, relation to hide 53, 54
Sussex, hides recorded by Bede **50**, *51*

Tadlow, vill (Cambs.) 92, *94*
tax-farming 61
taxation
   Domesday in historic context of taxation 106–10, **107**
   potential tax implications for taxpayers in Cambridgeshire and Huntingdonshire 135, **136**
   see also 'Peter's pence'; poll taxes; quantum taxes; quota taxes; valuation lists
tenants-in-chief
   geographical ownership patterns 27–9
   hierarchy of demesnes 8–9, **8**
   listed in Domesday 18, **34**
   and logistics of Domesday 89, 91–2, 94
   as primary taxpayers 25, 30, 135, **136**
terms of reference 31–3
   boroughs 79
terriers *see* estate management
Thanet, Isle of (Kent), hides recorded by Bede 49, **50**, *51*
Thriplow Hundred (Cambs.) 90, 92
timber, standing 45, 47, 48
timescale for compiling Domesday 13, 101–2, 114
   timetable 85–104, **103**, **104**, 111–12
tithe 9, 43, 56, 106, 145
title
   changes 26
   disputes 18
   see also legal ownership; possession
Torksey 80–3, **80**, *81*
Torrens system of land registration, Australia 17
Toseland Hundred (Hunts.)
   actual or potential ploughlands 63, **63**
   reduced hides 36
   Royal holdings 71
   study area 11, **11**
   survey entries 97
towns *see* boroughs
TRE (Tempore Regis Eduardi) values
   interpretation 72–4, **73**, 76
   in typical Domesday entry **34**

urban centres *see* boroughs
USA 30, 70 (Box 6)

valuation 55–78
   see also rents and rental values; valuation lists
valuation lists
   Domesday as valuation list 21–2
   valuation list logistics **86**
   see also Rating system
Valuation Office *see* Inland Revenue, Valuation Office
valuere and variants, use in Domesday 60
vif-gages 61
villagers categorised in social class, in typical Domesday entry **34**
vills
   named in typical Domesday entry **34**
   as unit for tax assessment 9, 25
Vitruvius 117n4

waste (unused or devastated land) 21, 56, 63, 66, 71, 73, 125
watermills **34**, 35, 41, 42, 60–1, 66, 83, 105, **141**
   Cambridge 83, 91, **142**
Weeting, vill (Norfolk) **141**
Wendy, vill (Cambs.) 28, **28**, 92, *94*
Whaddon, vill (Cambs.) 28, **28**, 92, *94*
Whittlesey Mere (Hunts.) 46
Wight, Isle of, hides recorded by Bede 49, **50**, *51*
Wilburton, vill (Cambs.) **141**
William I, King
   taxation policy 15, 20, 22, 24, 76, 110
   and timescale for Domesday 101, 110, 111–12
   see also Royal holdings
Wimblington, vill (Cambs.) **141**
Winchester (Hants.) 66, *67*, 88
   omitted from Domesday 84
Winchester, bishop of, as landholder in Cambridgeshire **136**
window taxes 70 (Box 6)
Witchford, vill (Cambs.) **141**
woodland 45–8
   Cornwall 47, 137, **137**, 138
   labour requirements for woodland management 123
   in typical Domesday entry **34**
woodland pasture 32–3, **34**, 45, 46–7, 69, 110, 123, 128, **133**, 134
writing materials **88**
Wulfmur of Eaton xiii (Box 1)

York 80–2, **80**, *81*
Yorkshire, TRE assessments 73
Young, Arthur 129

Index by Ann Hudson